CAMPING
STAINED GLASS
COLORING BOOK

LARGE PRINT

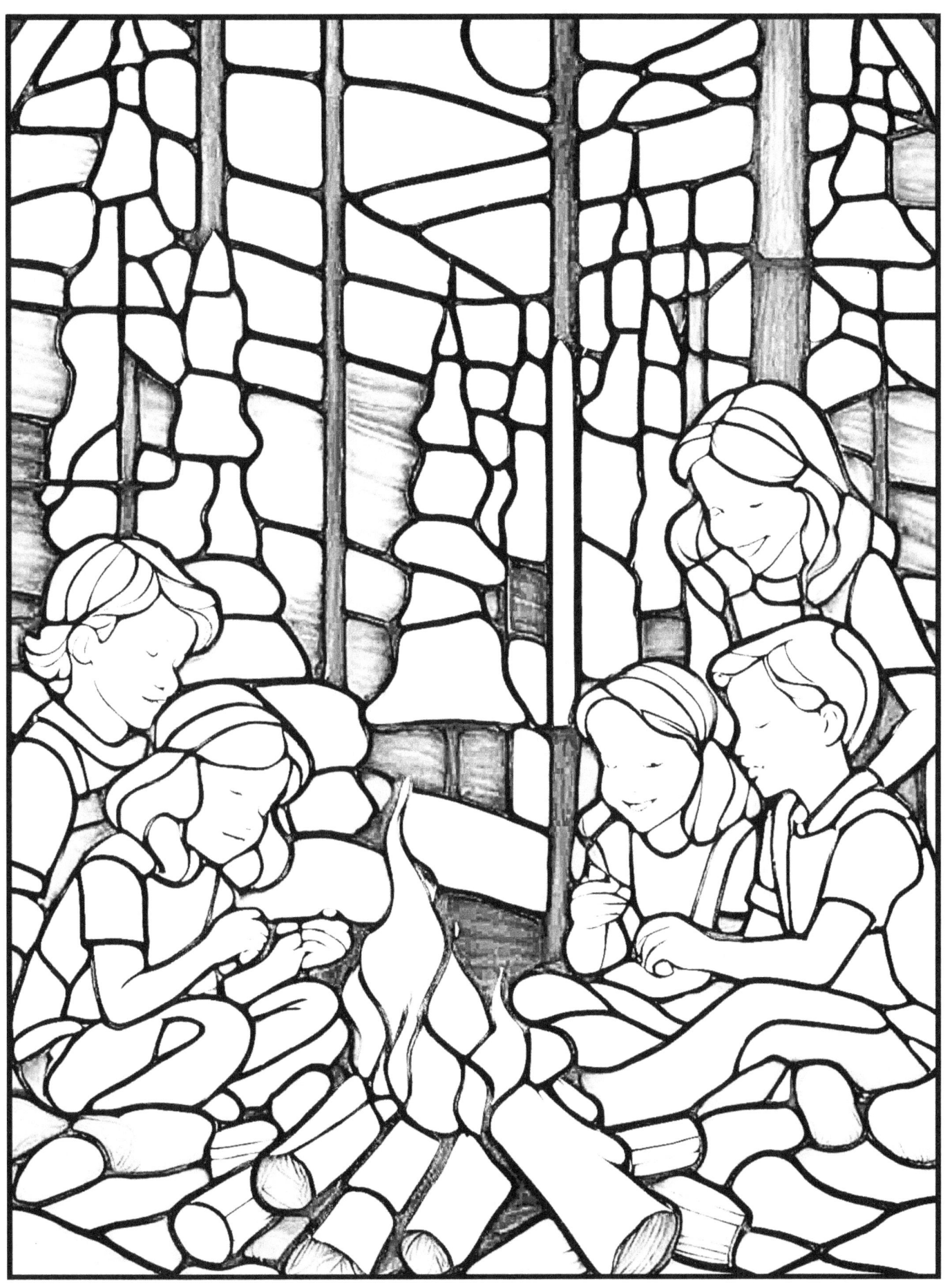

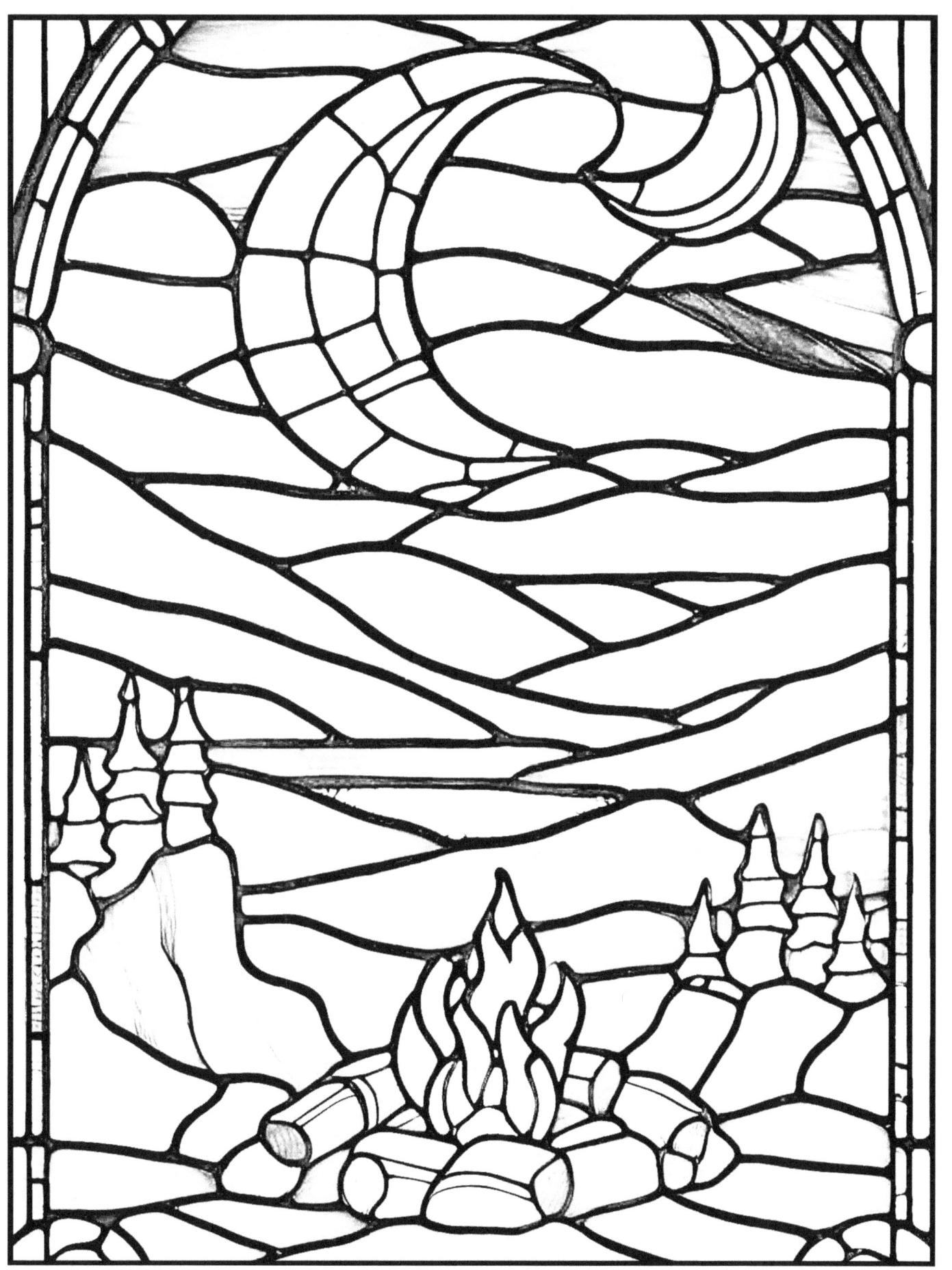

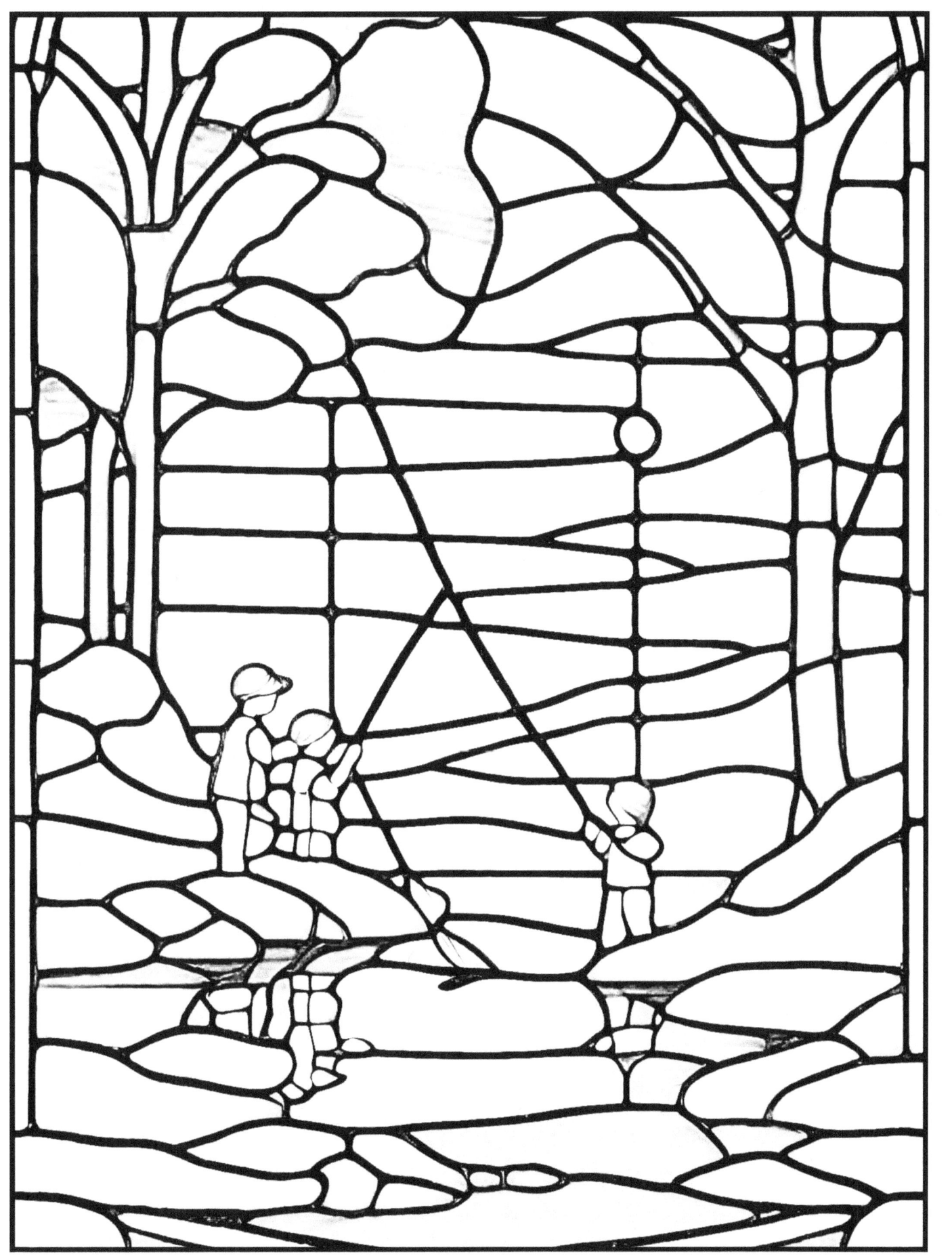

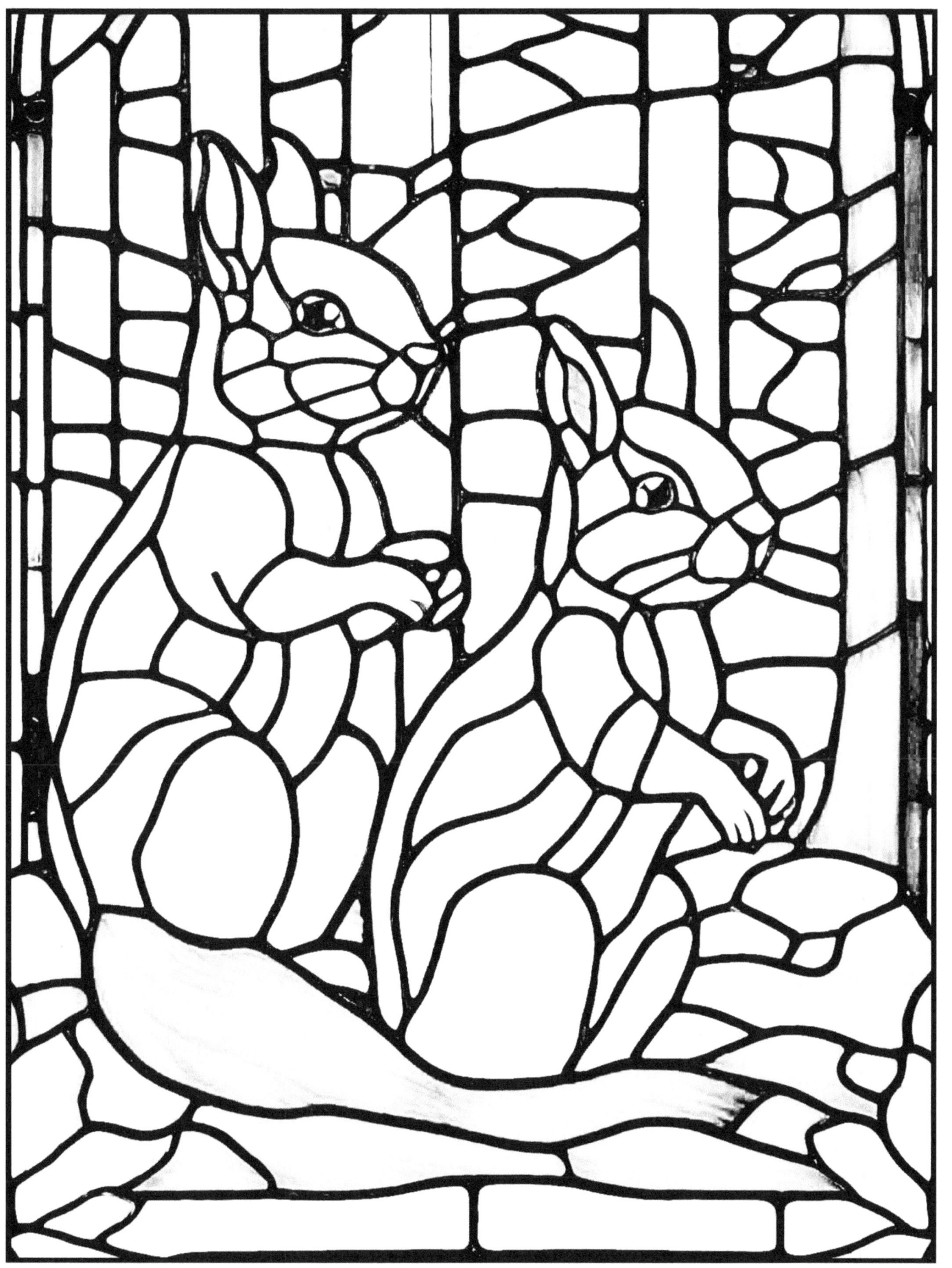

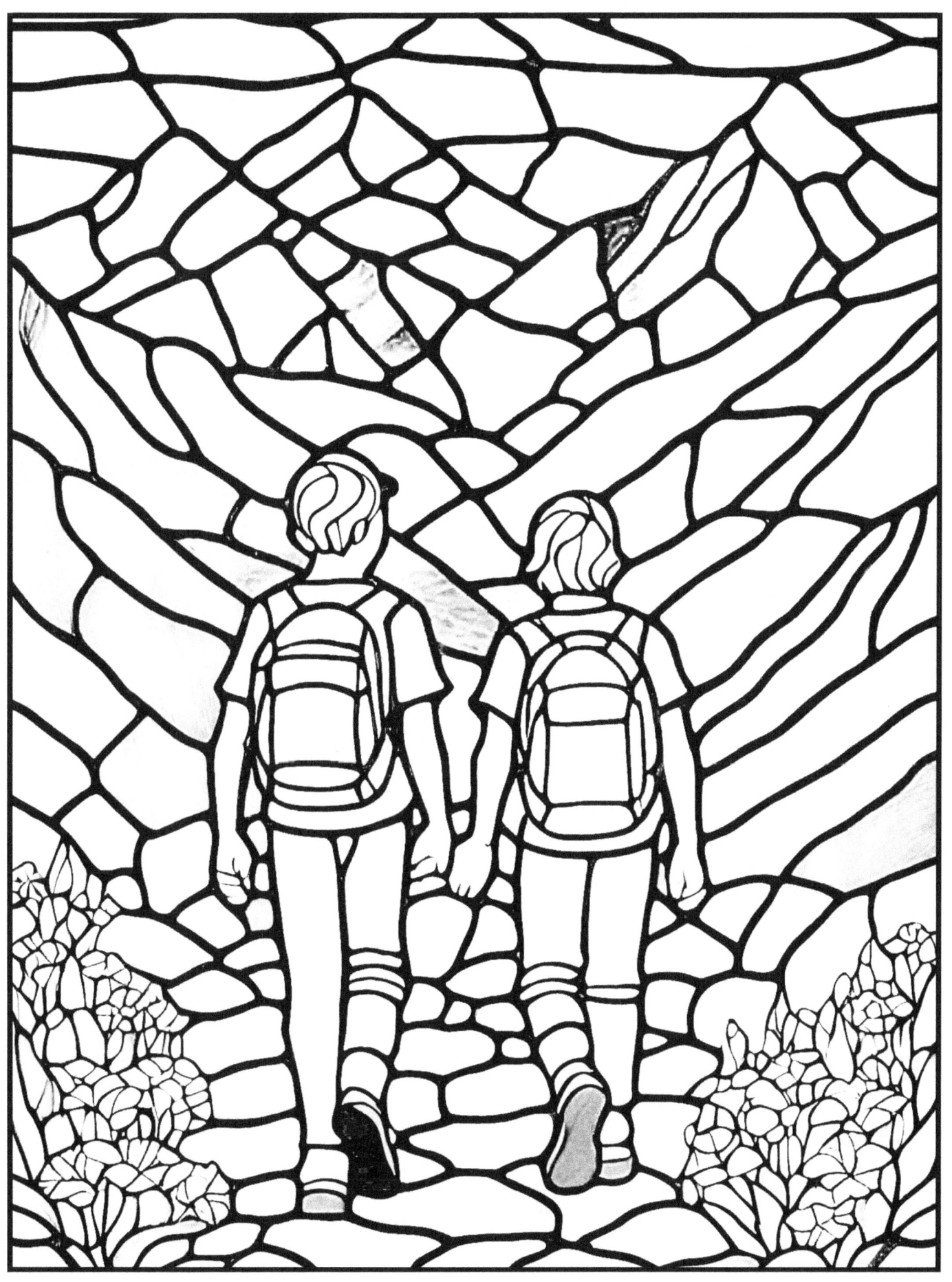

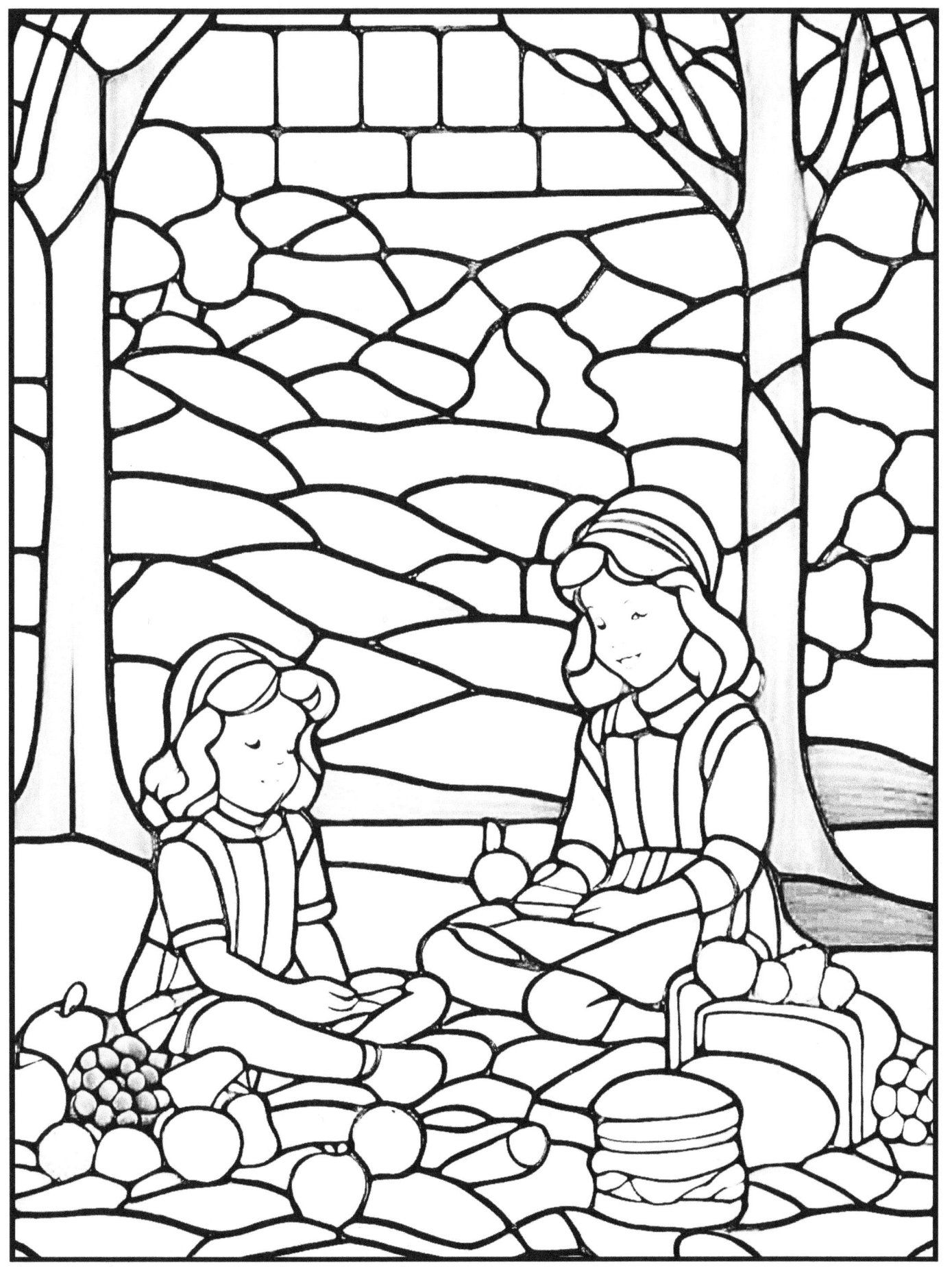

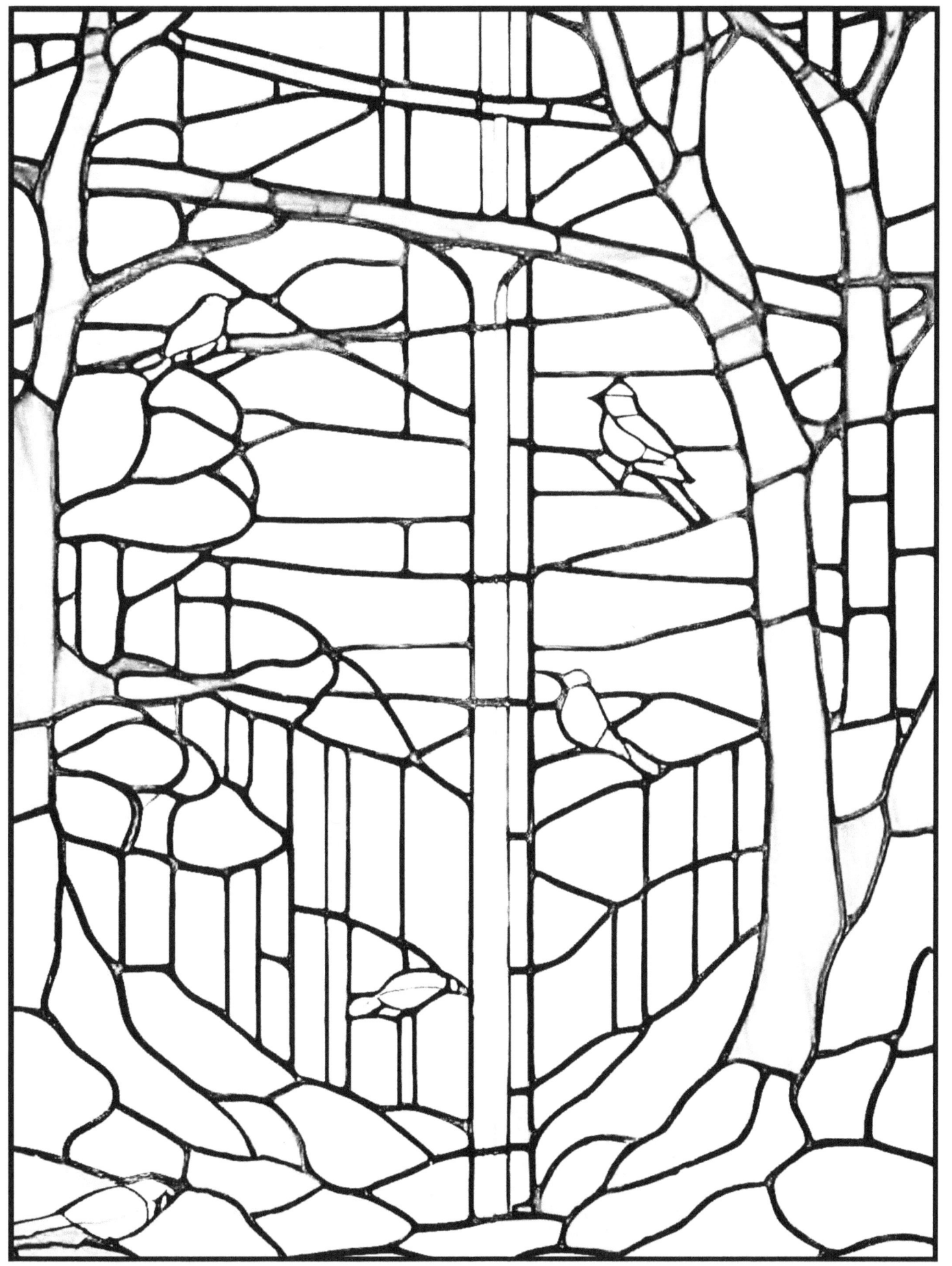

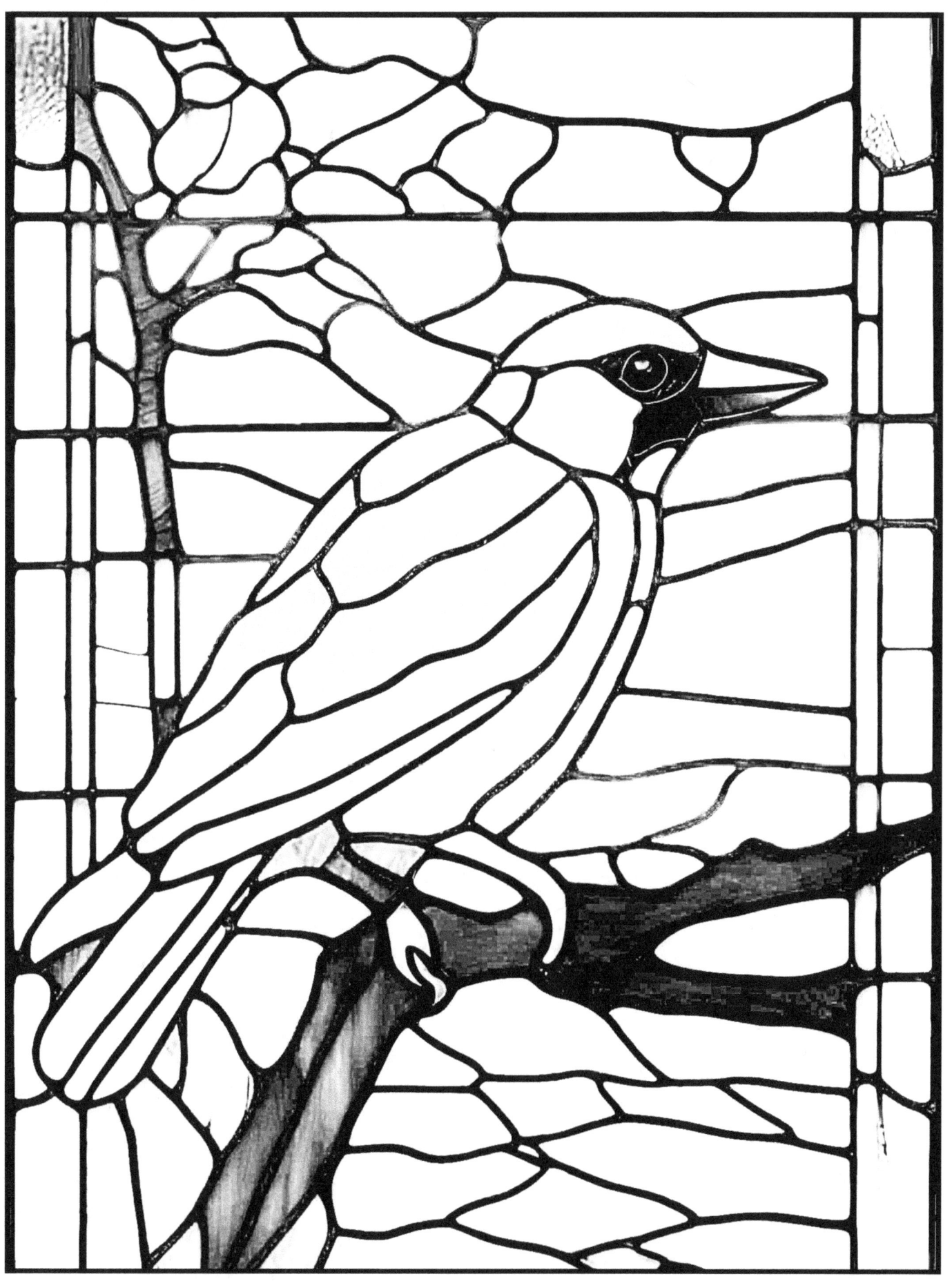

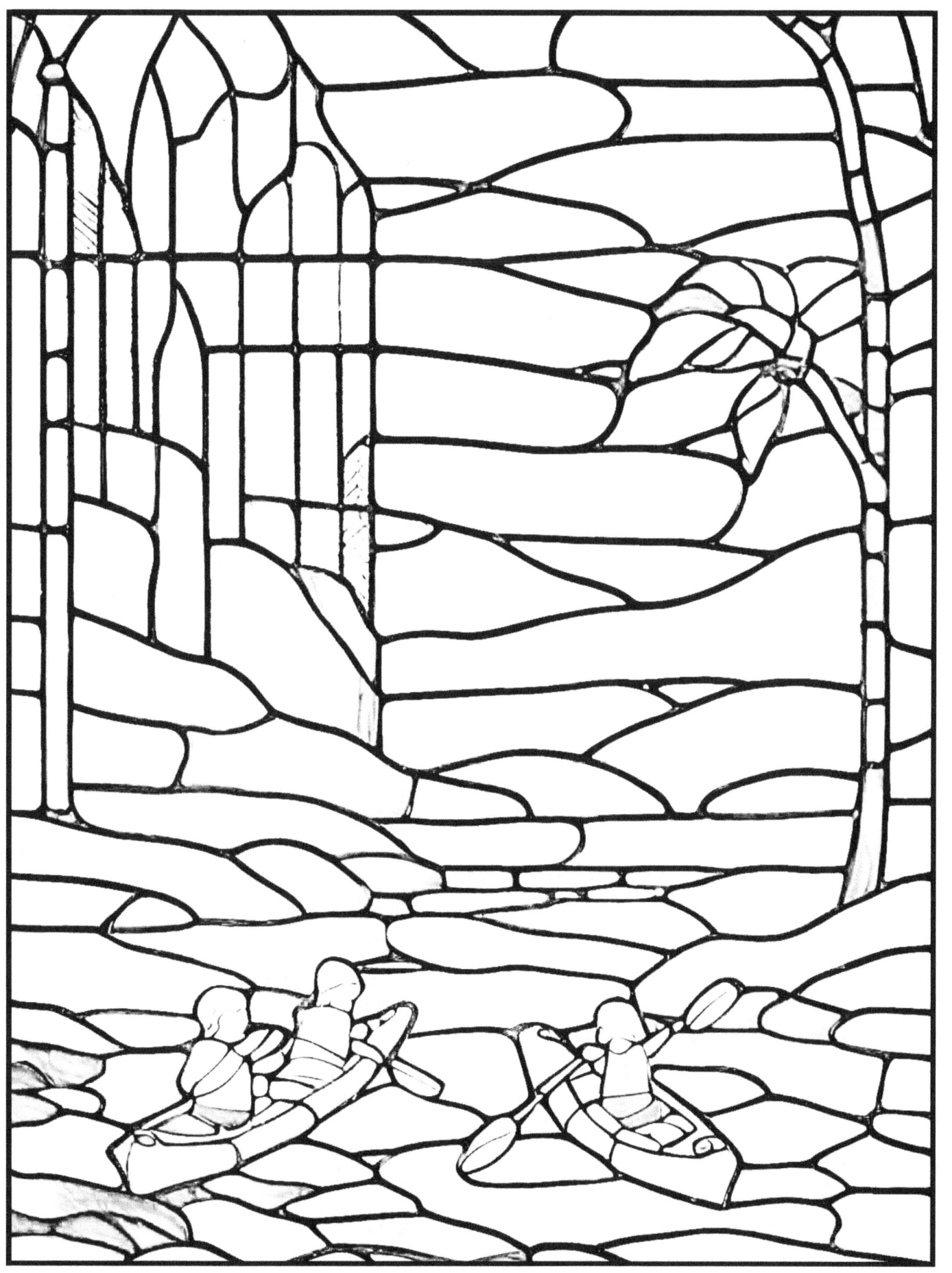

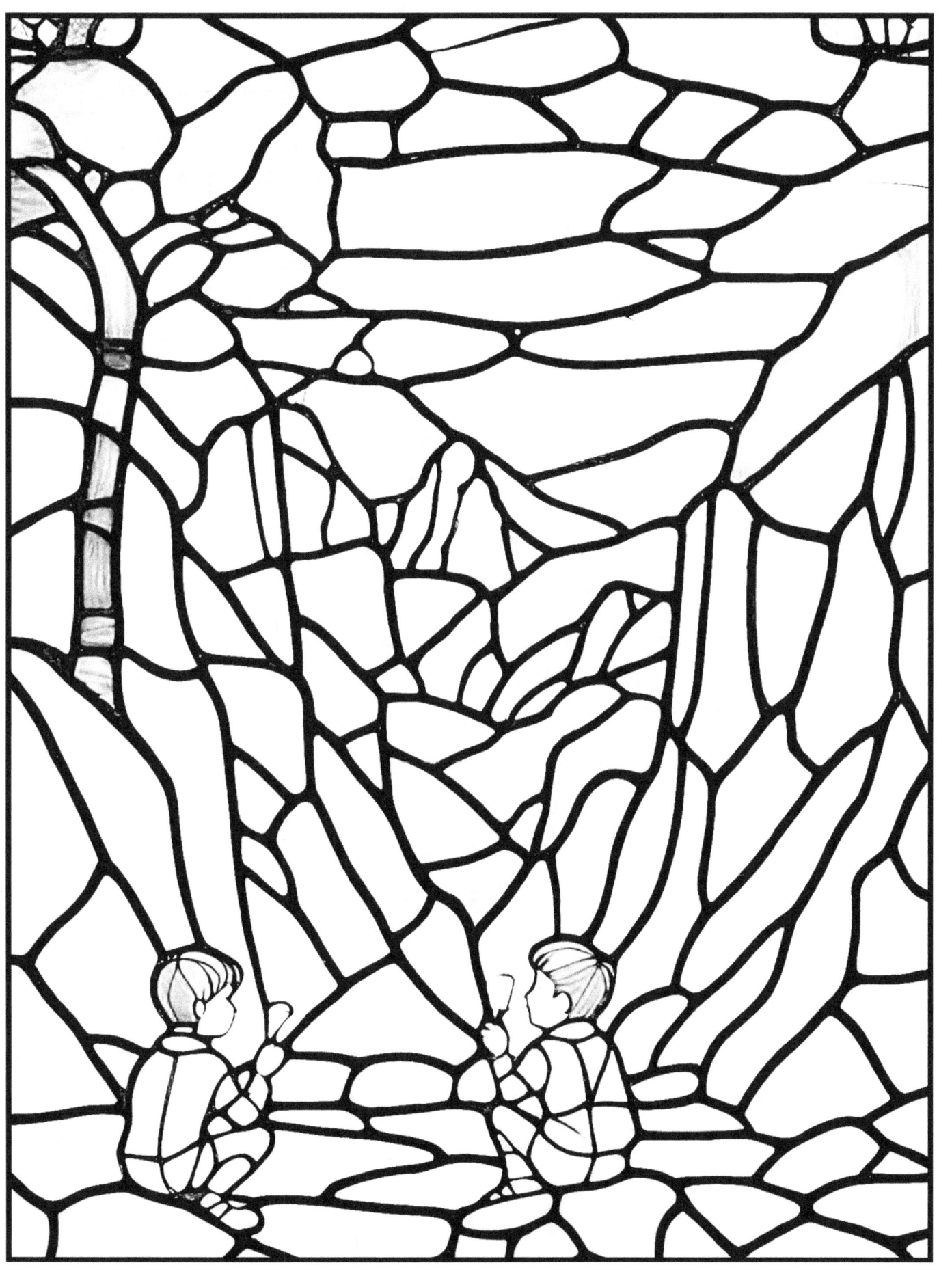

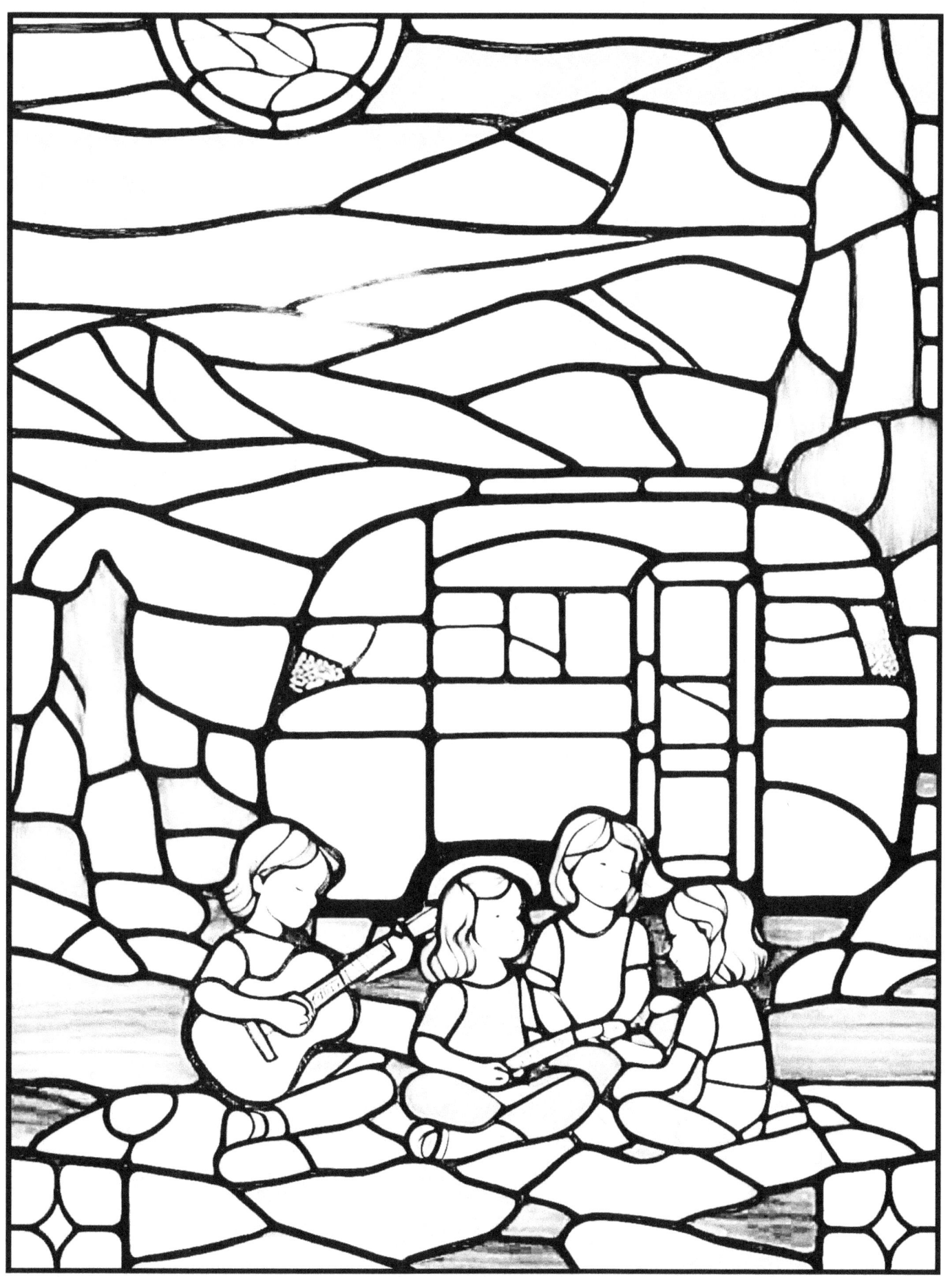

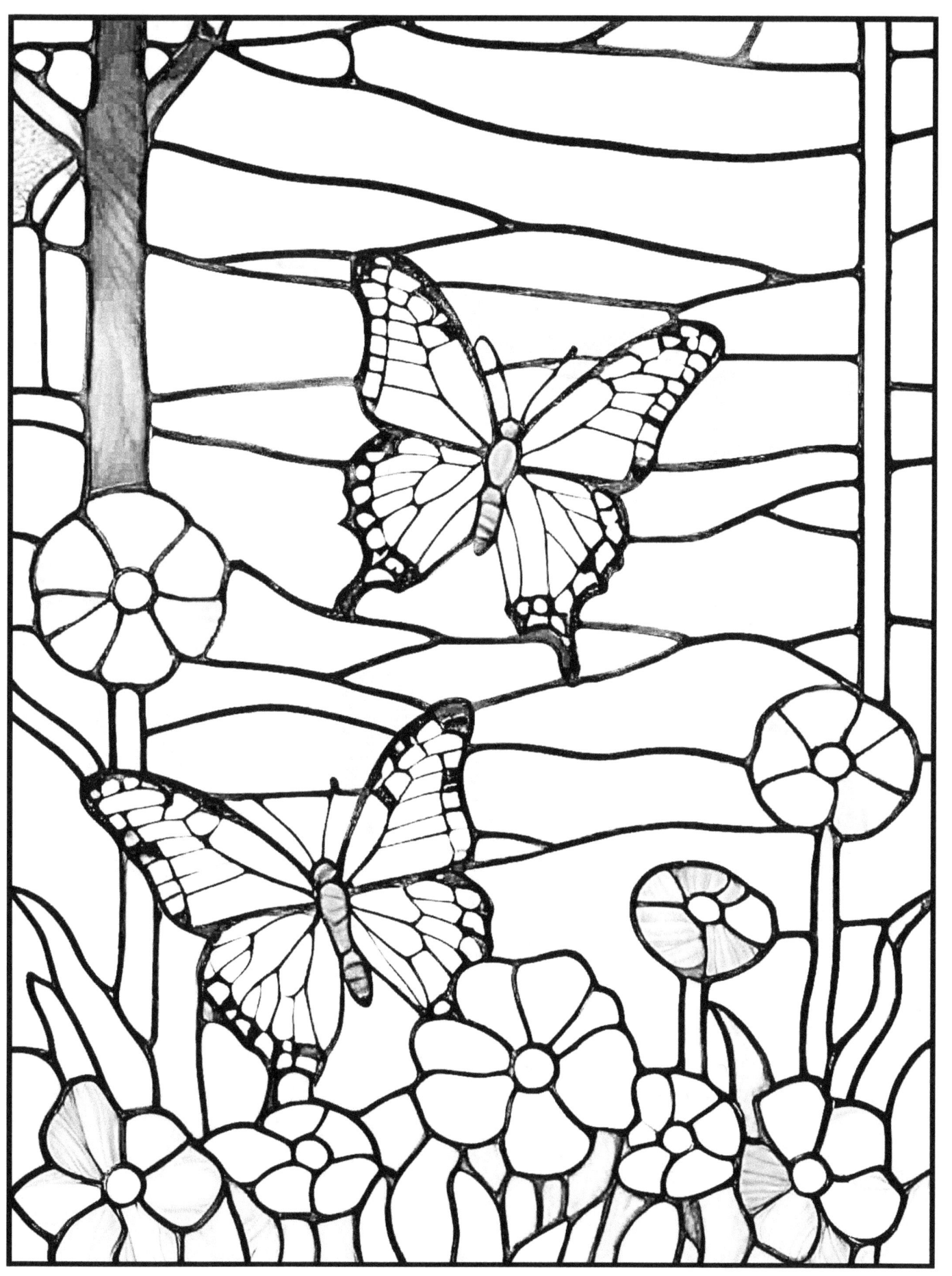

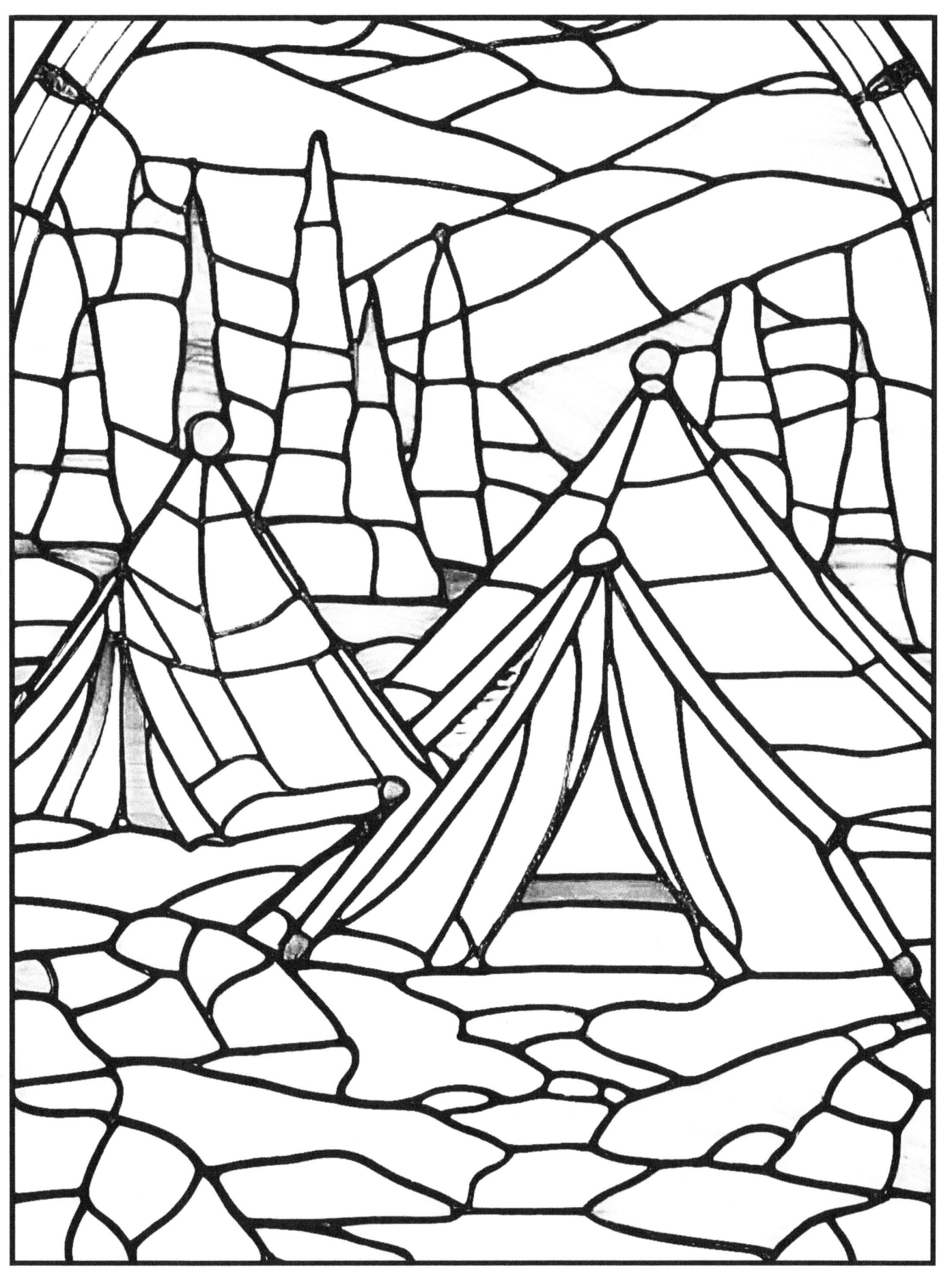

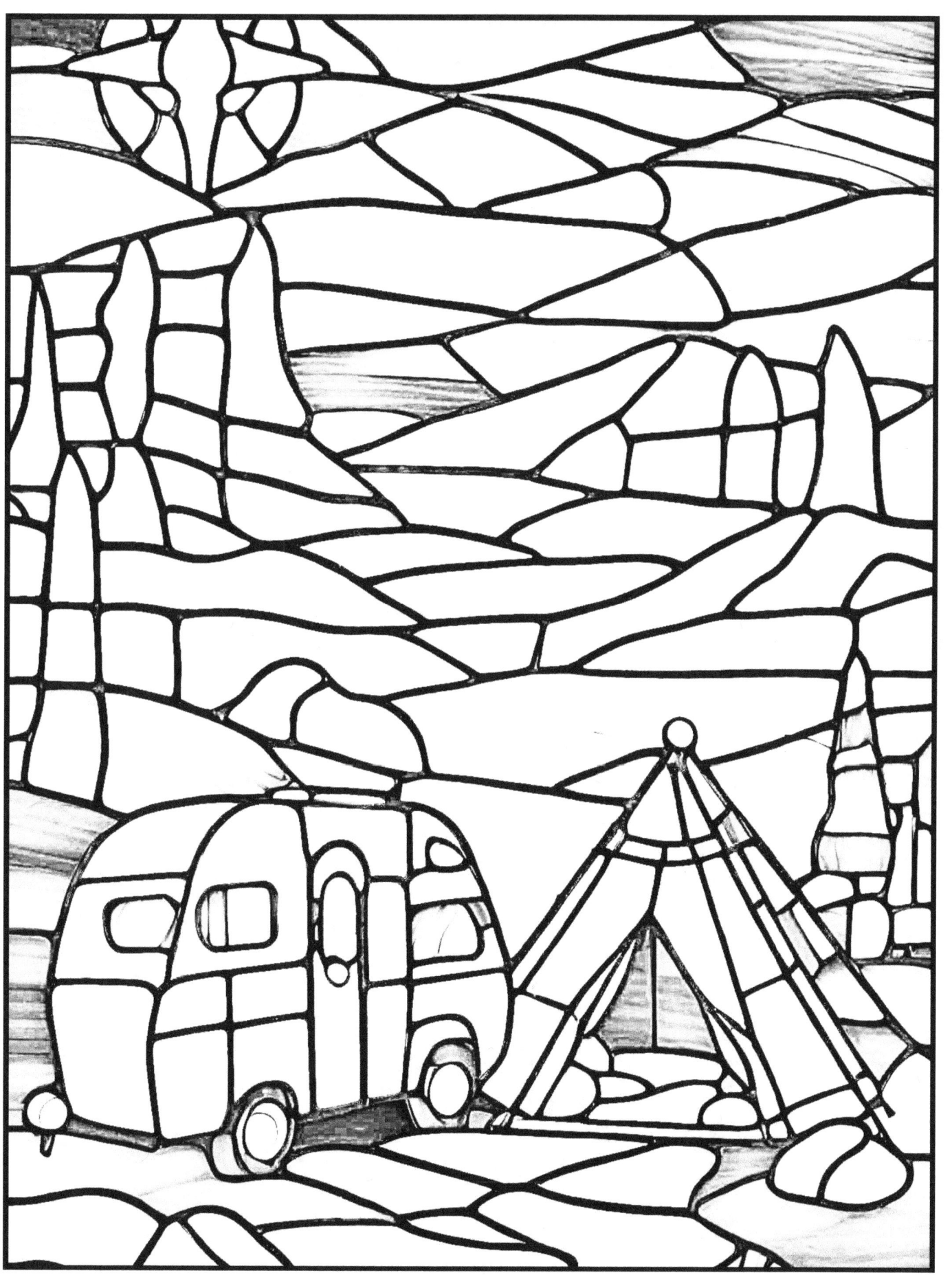

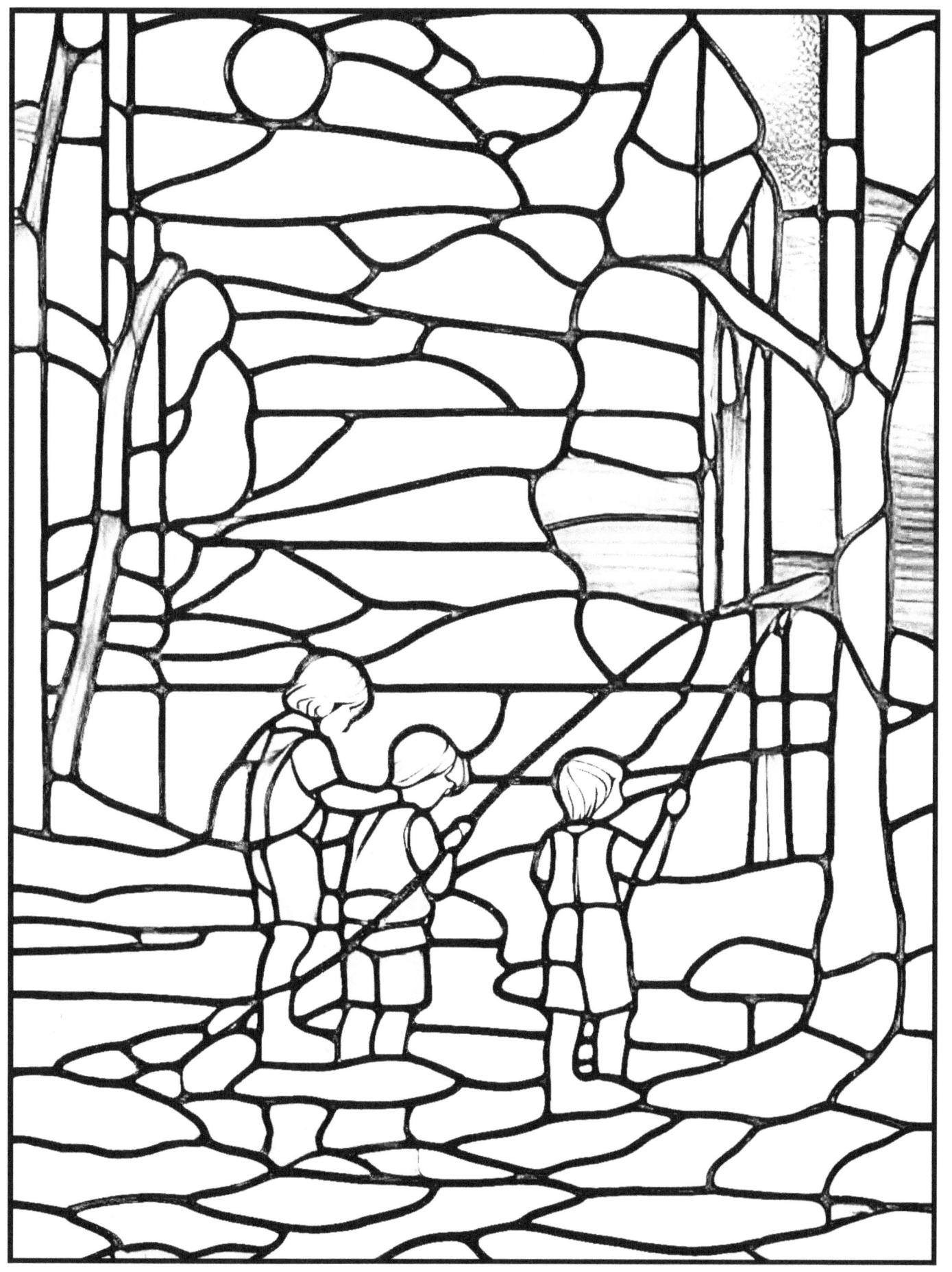

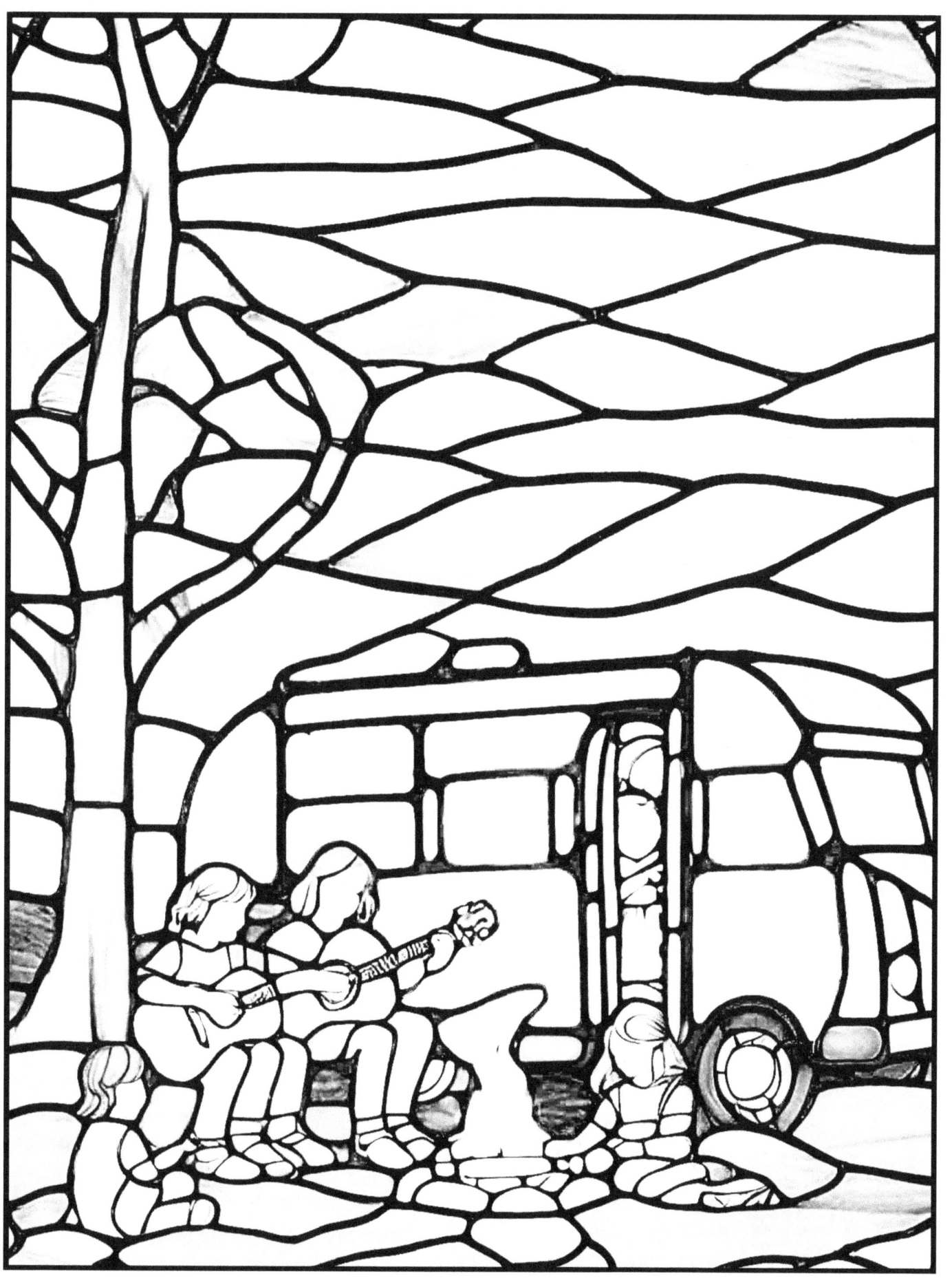

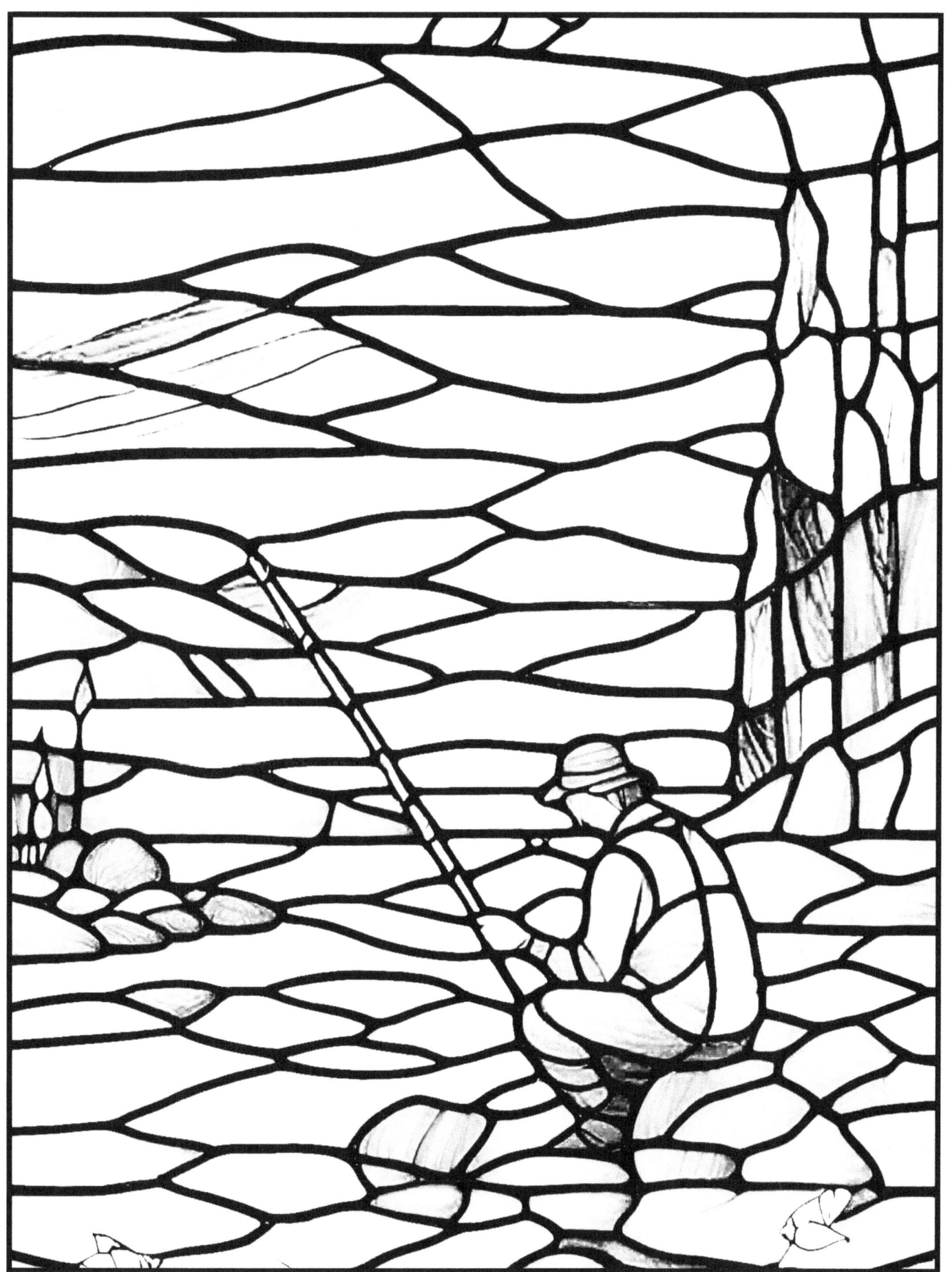

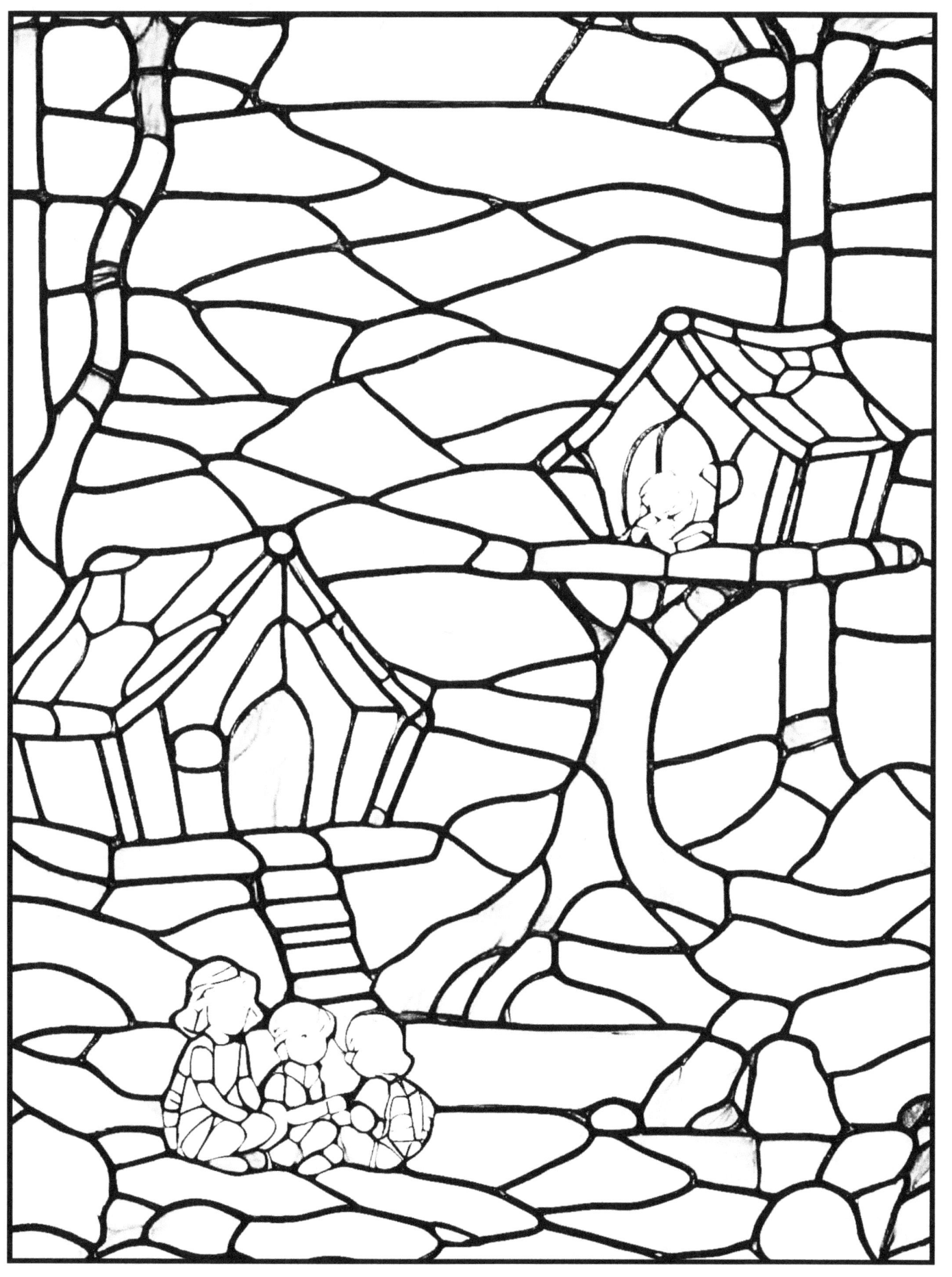

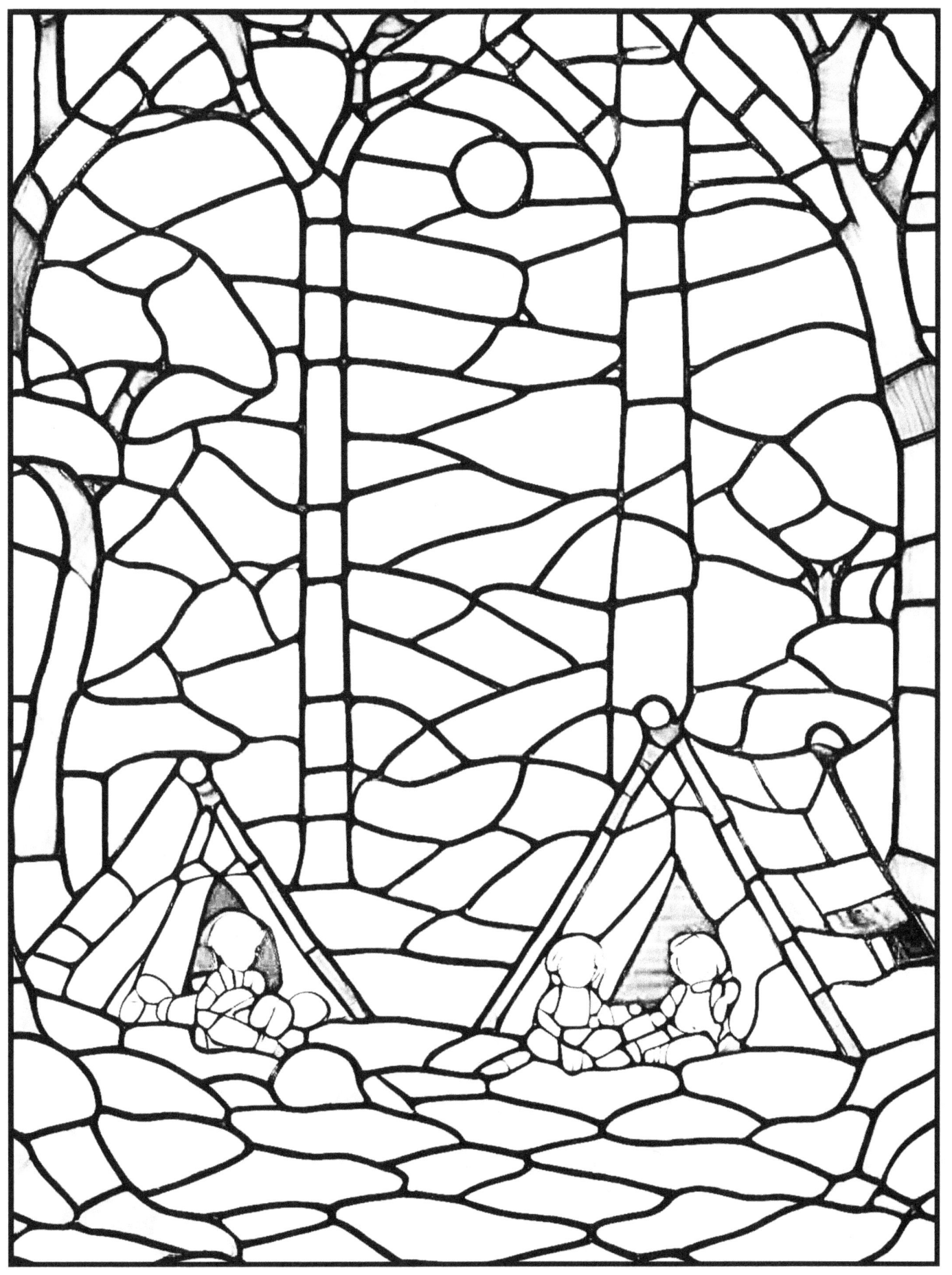

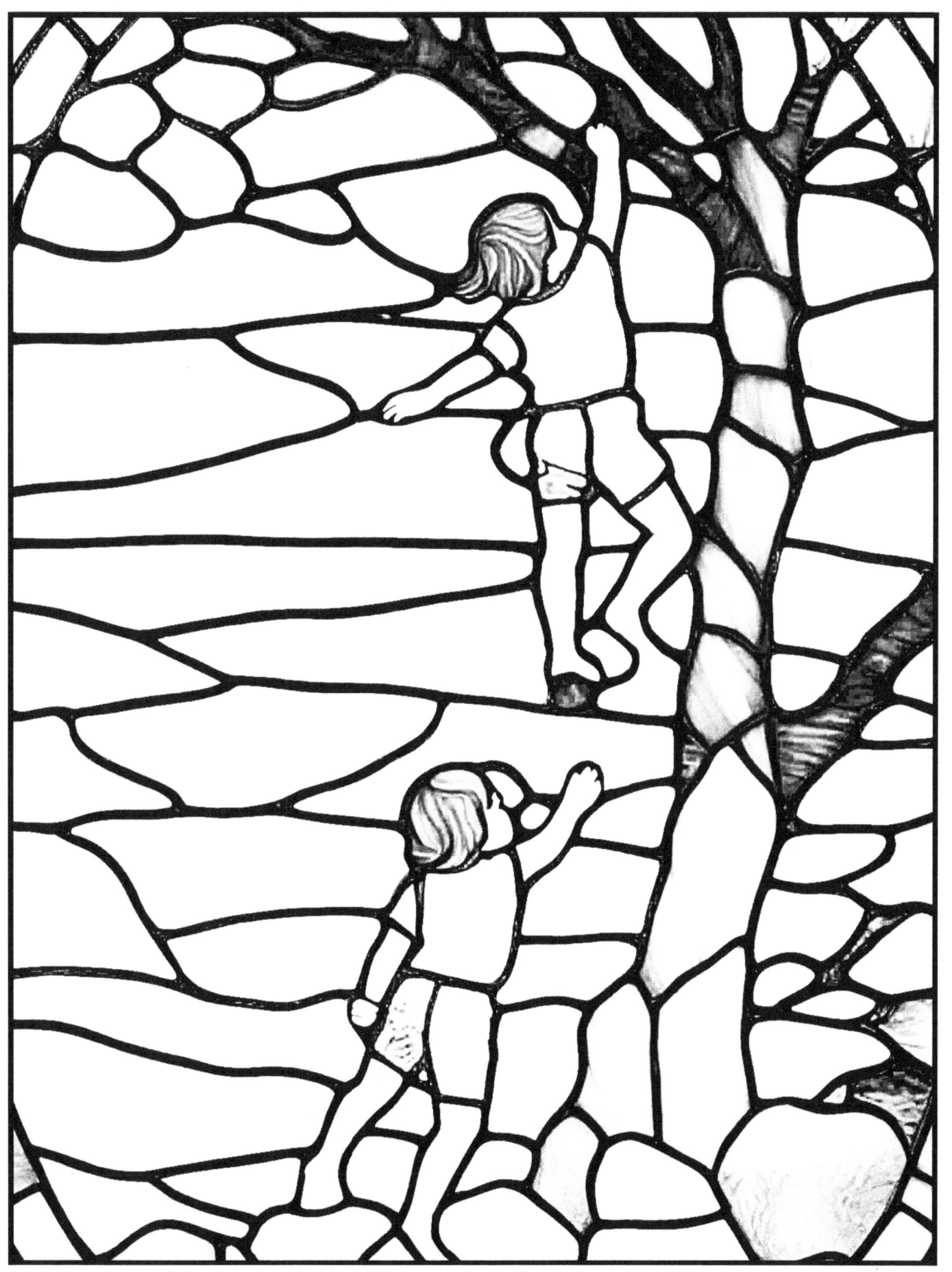

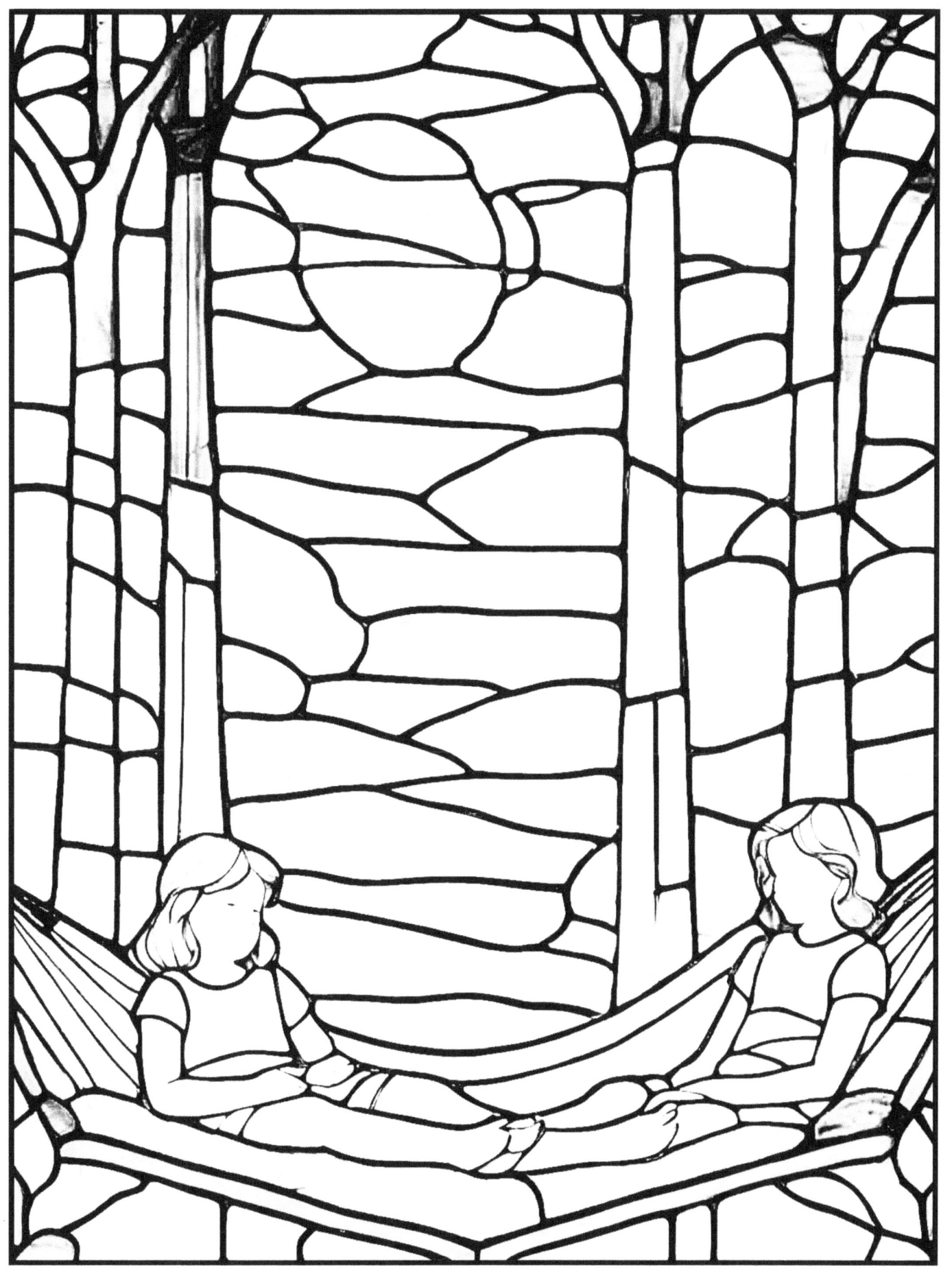

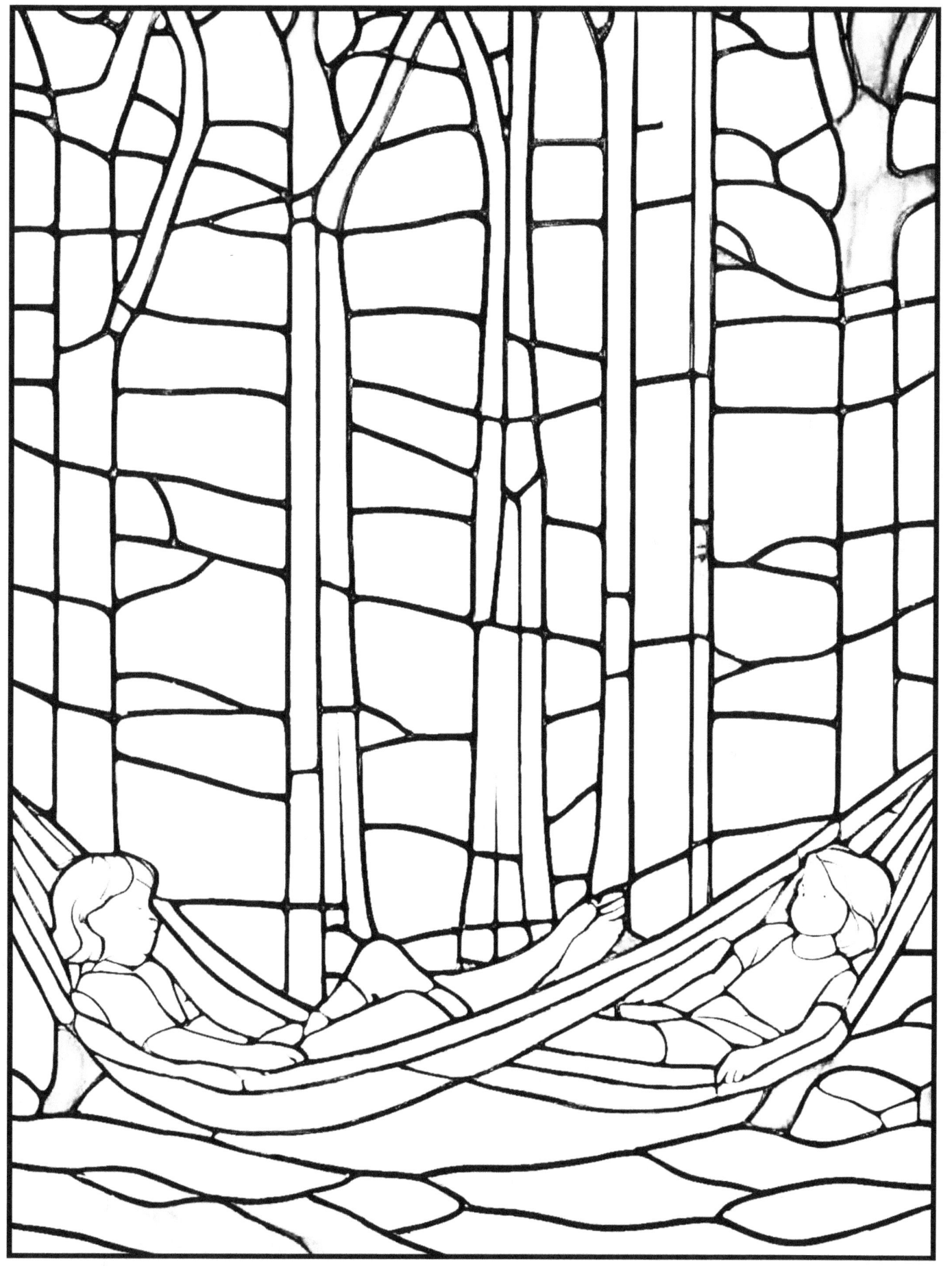

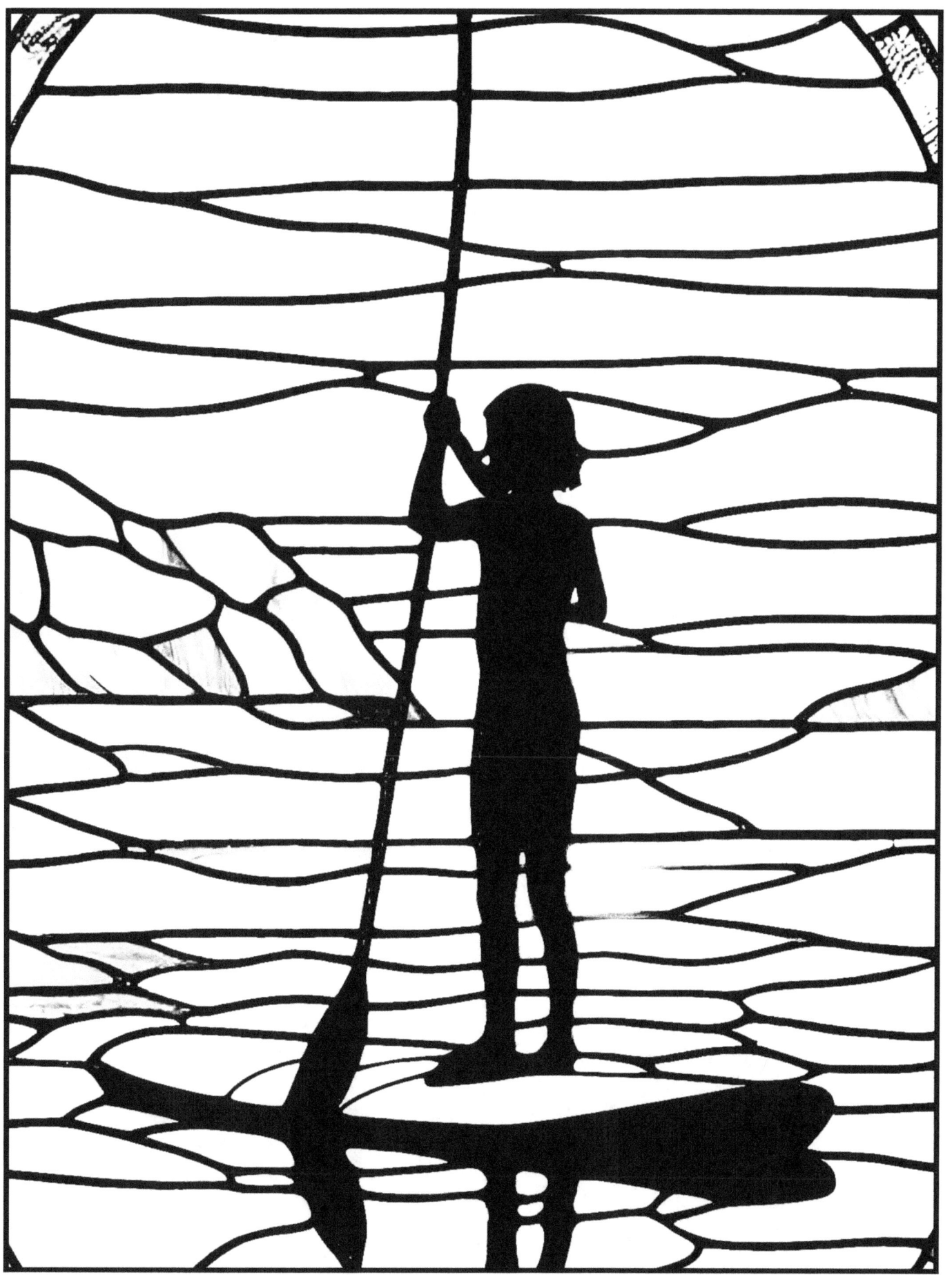

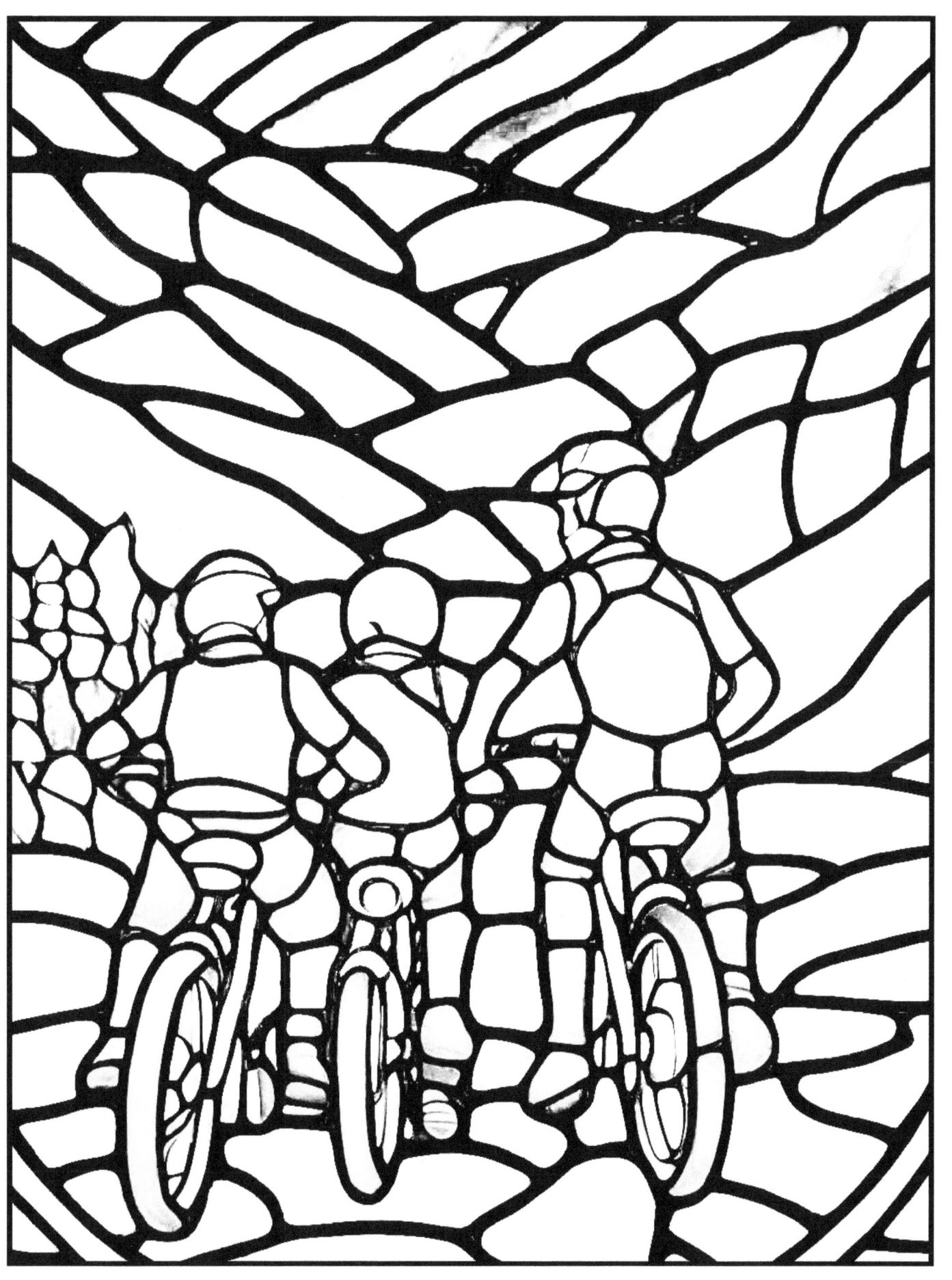

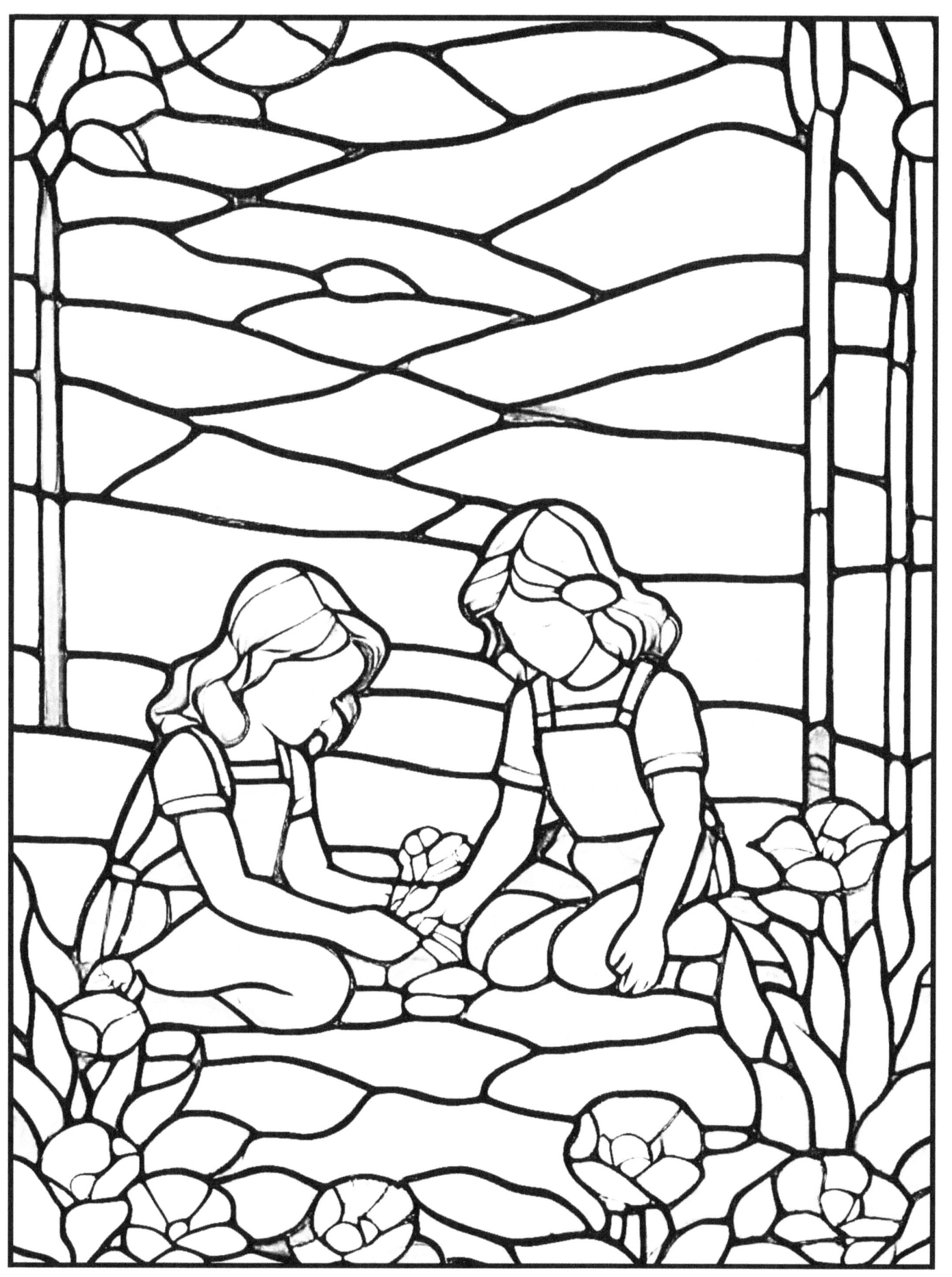

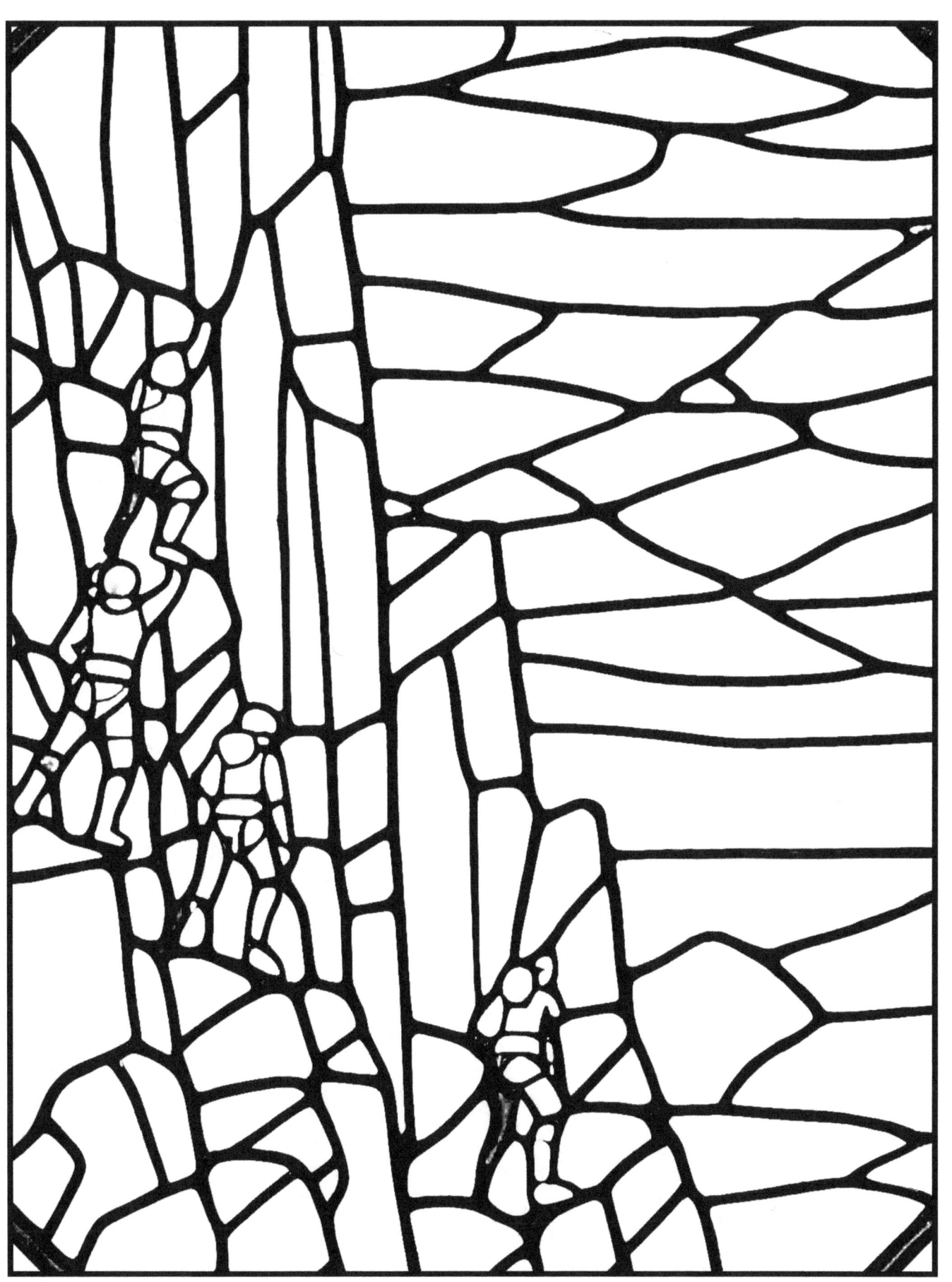

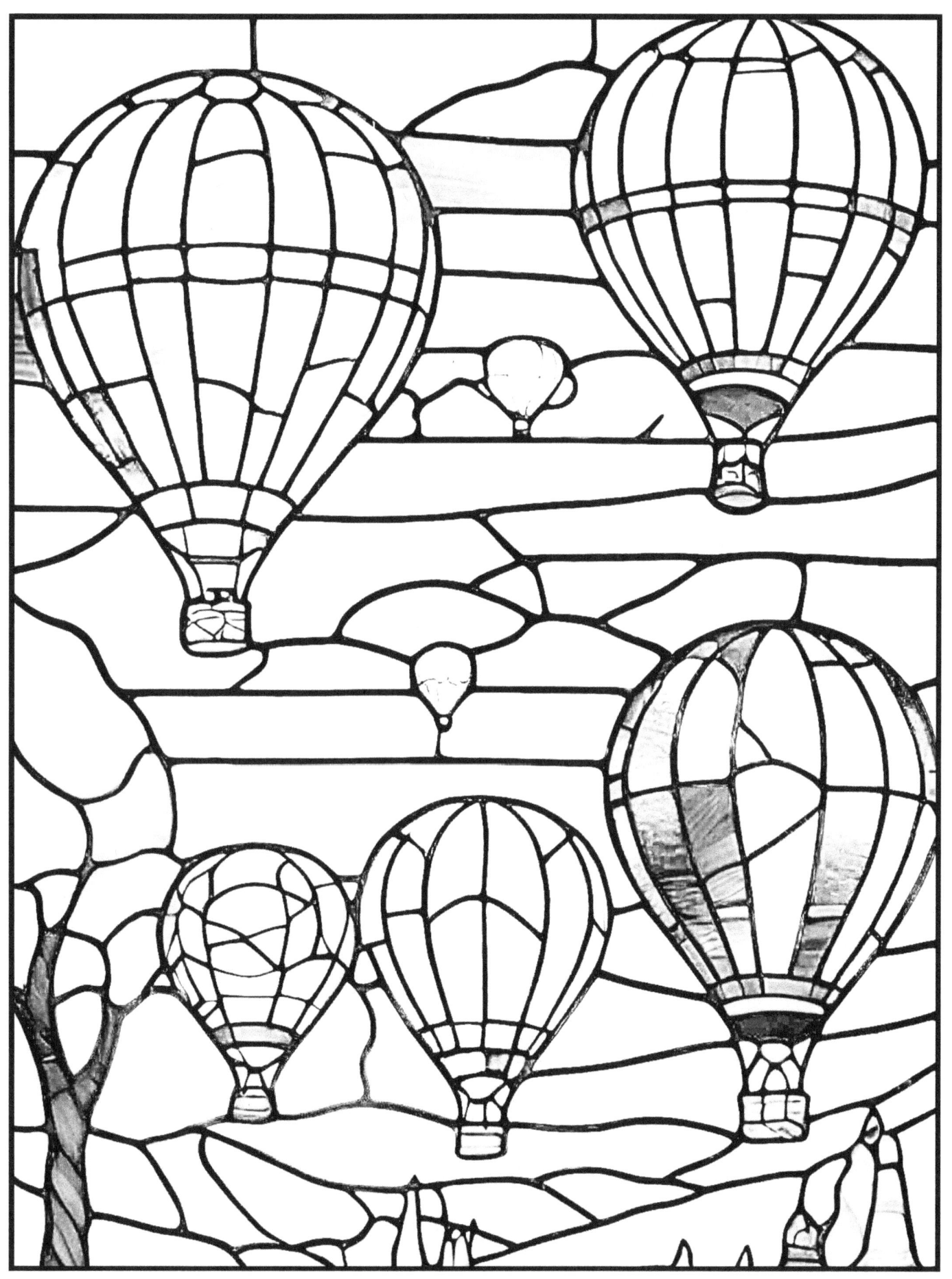

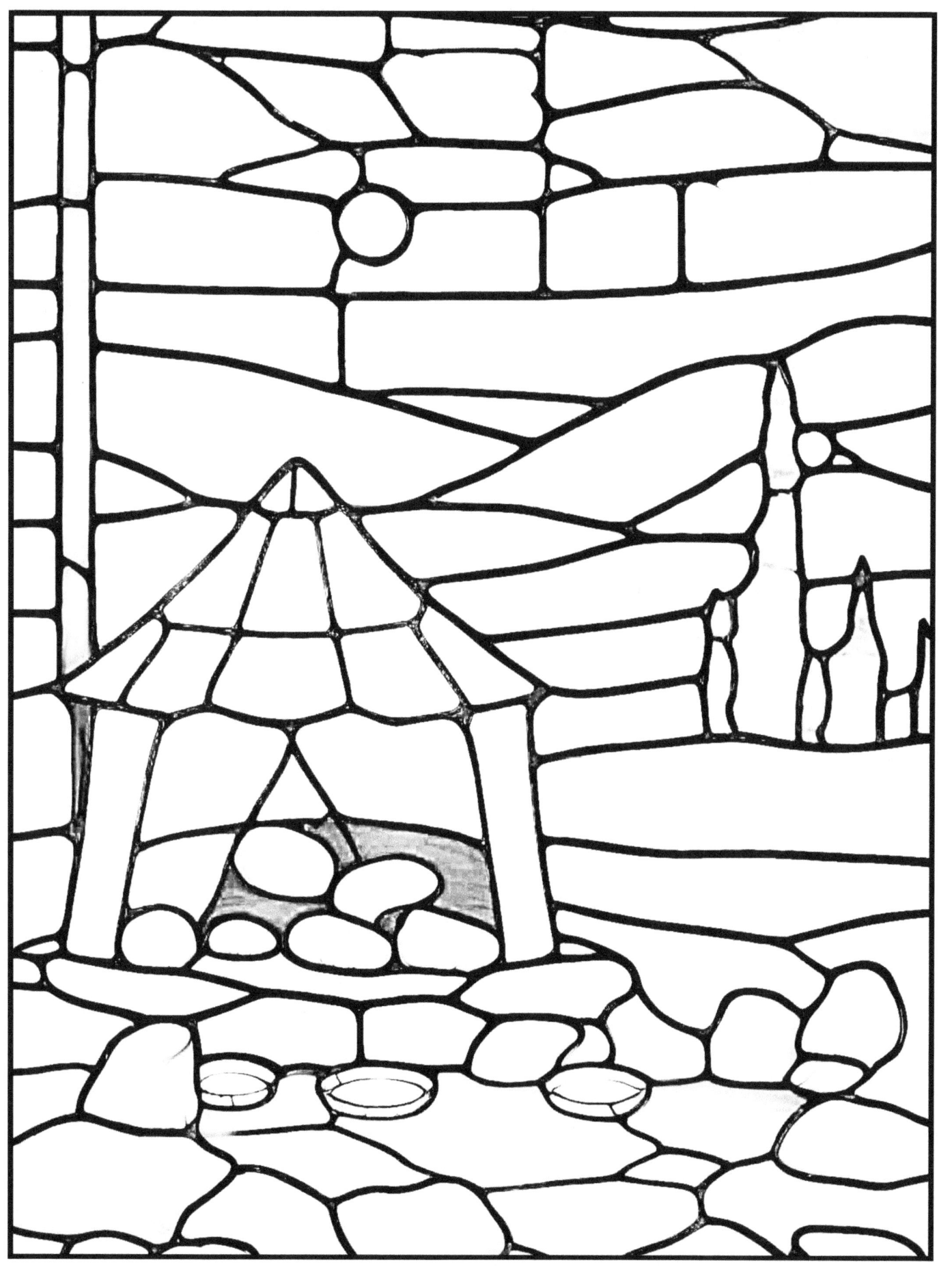

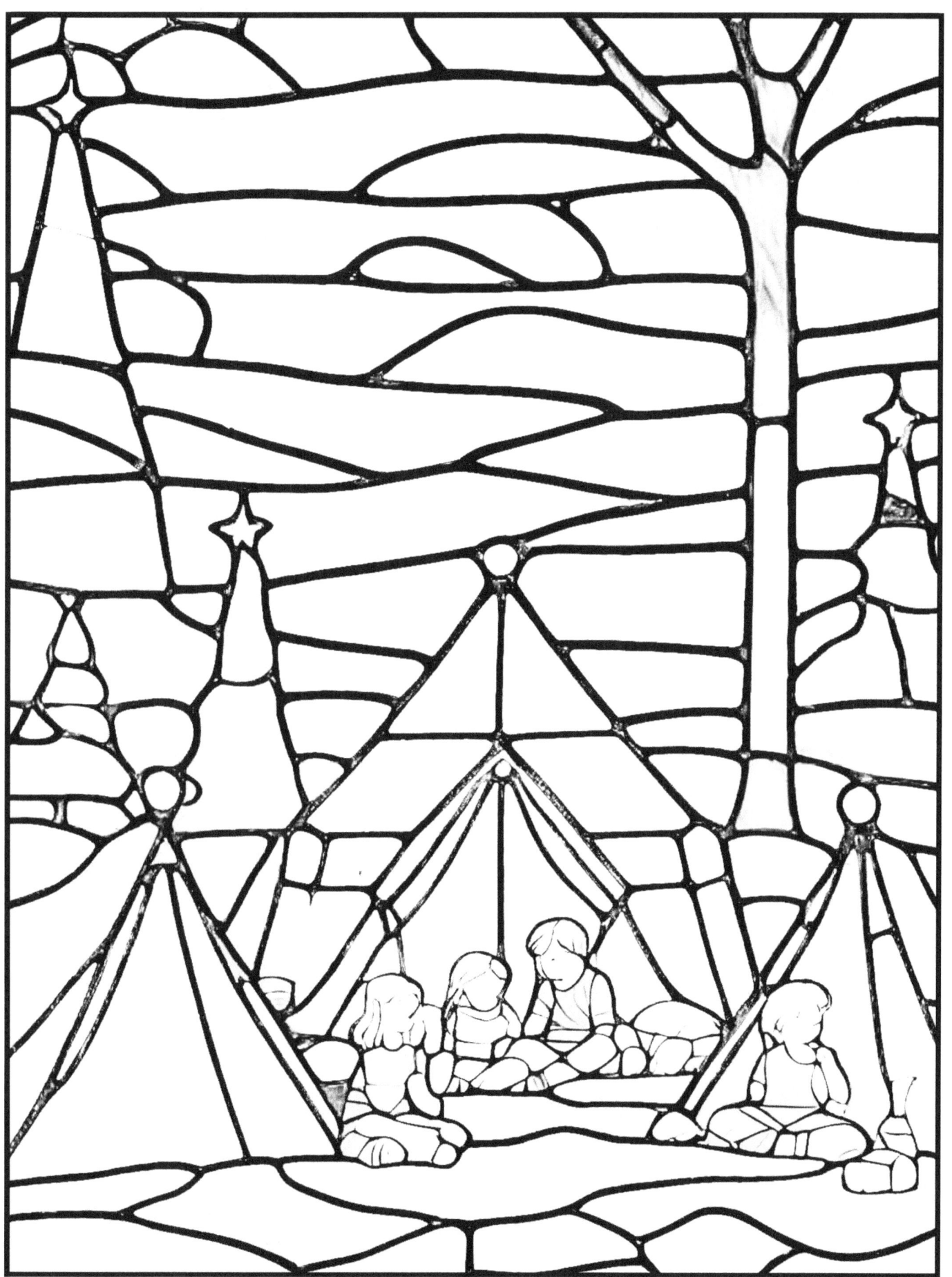

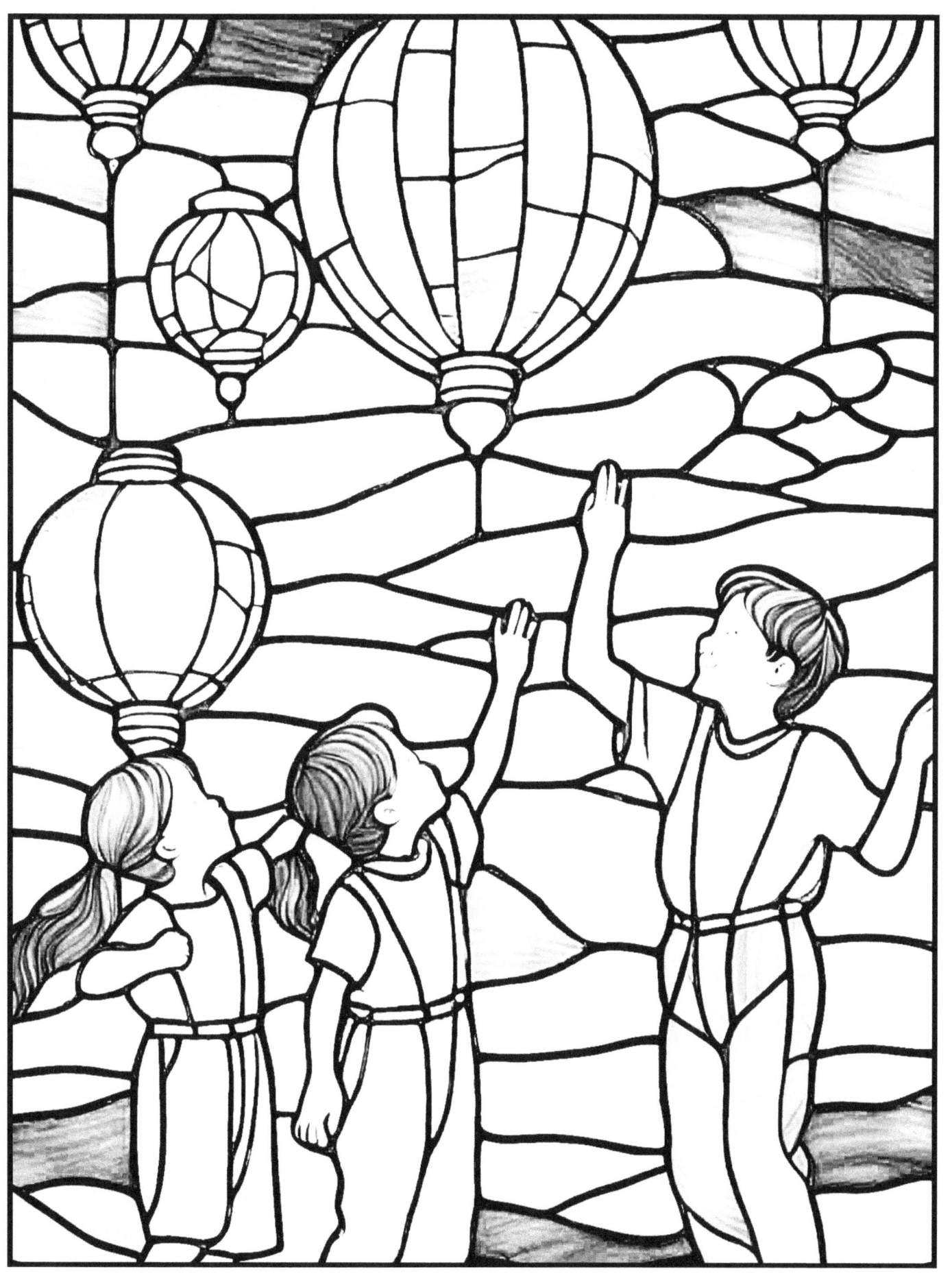

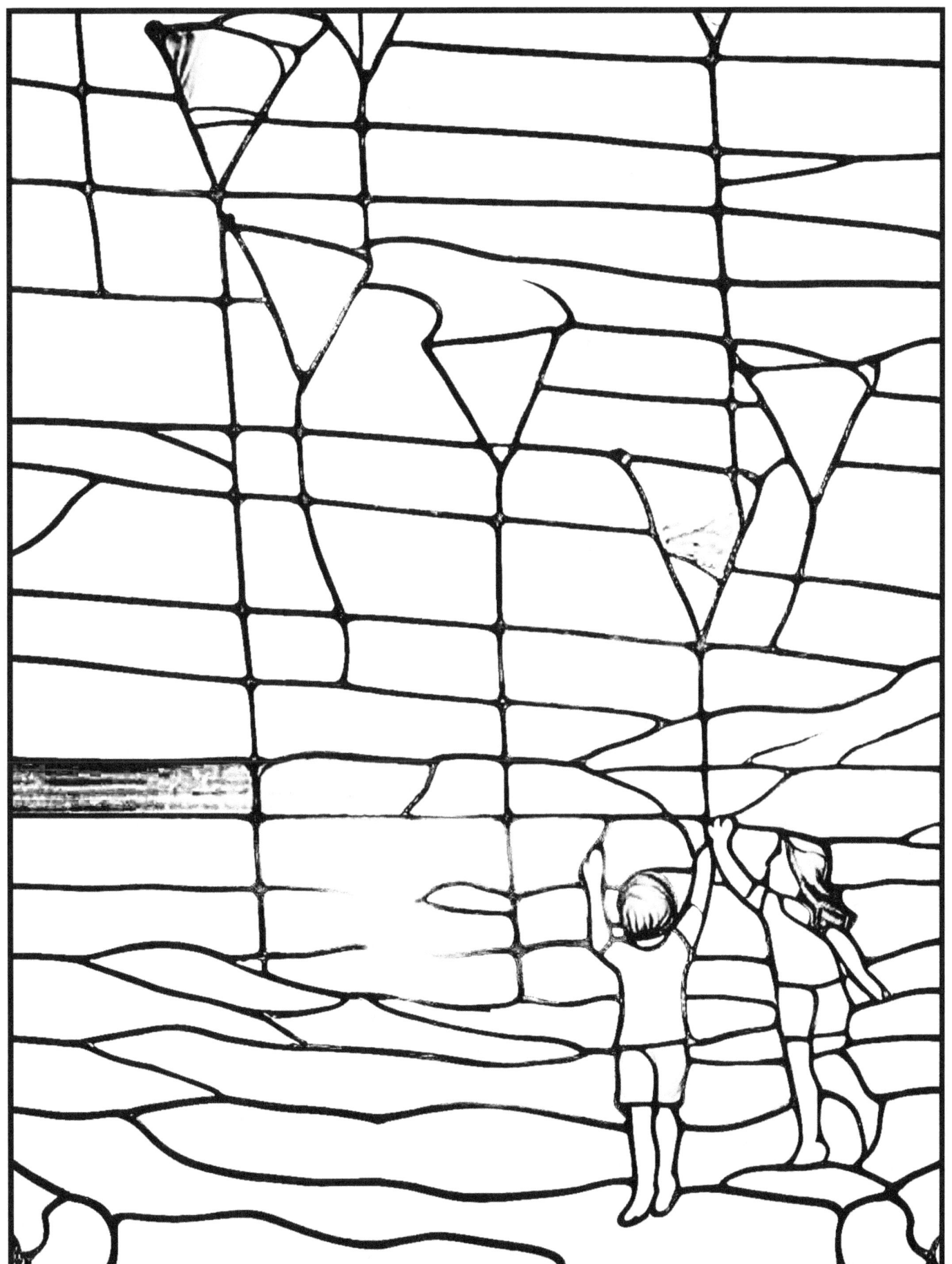

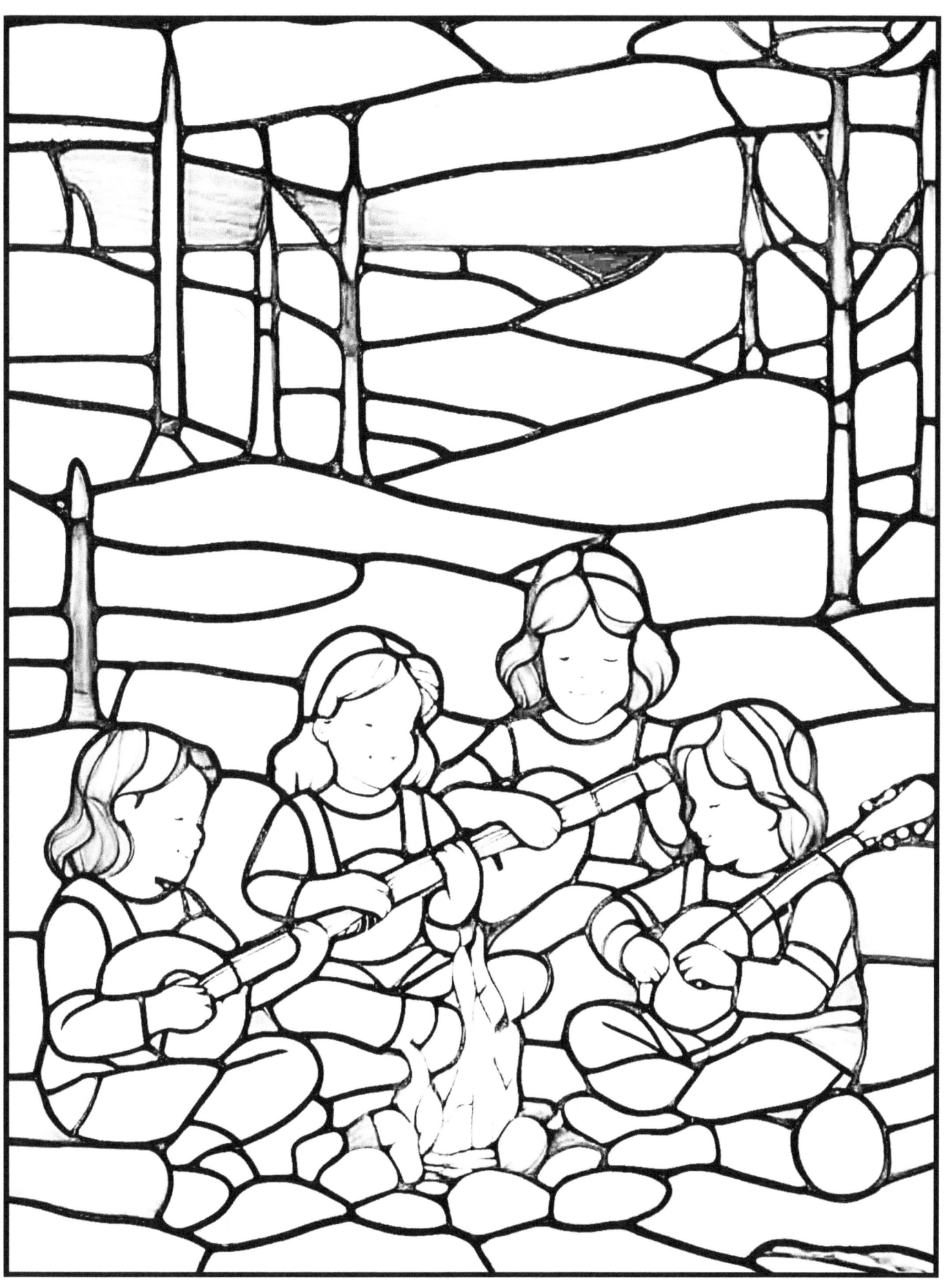

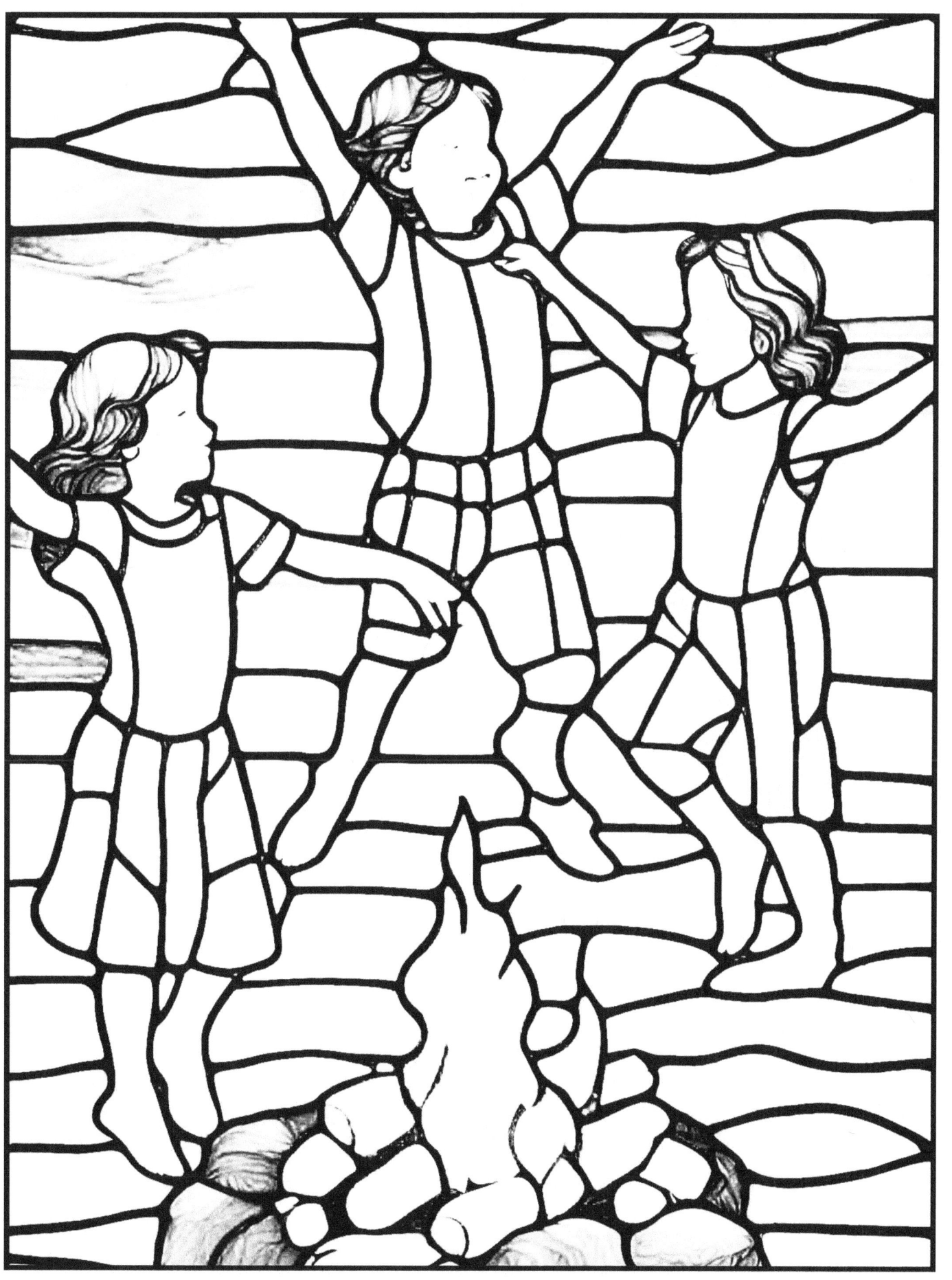

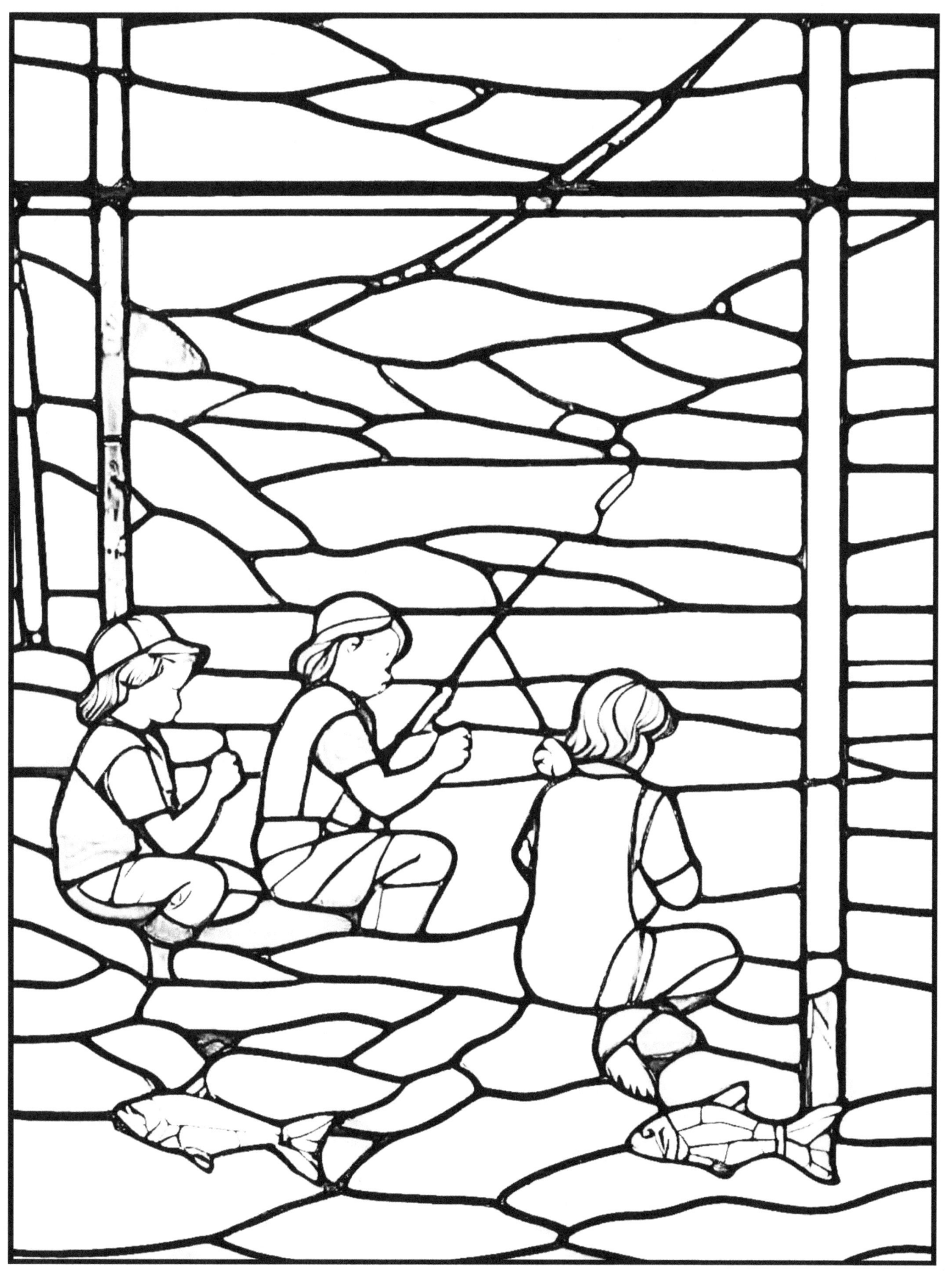

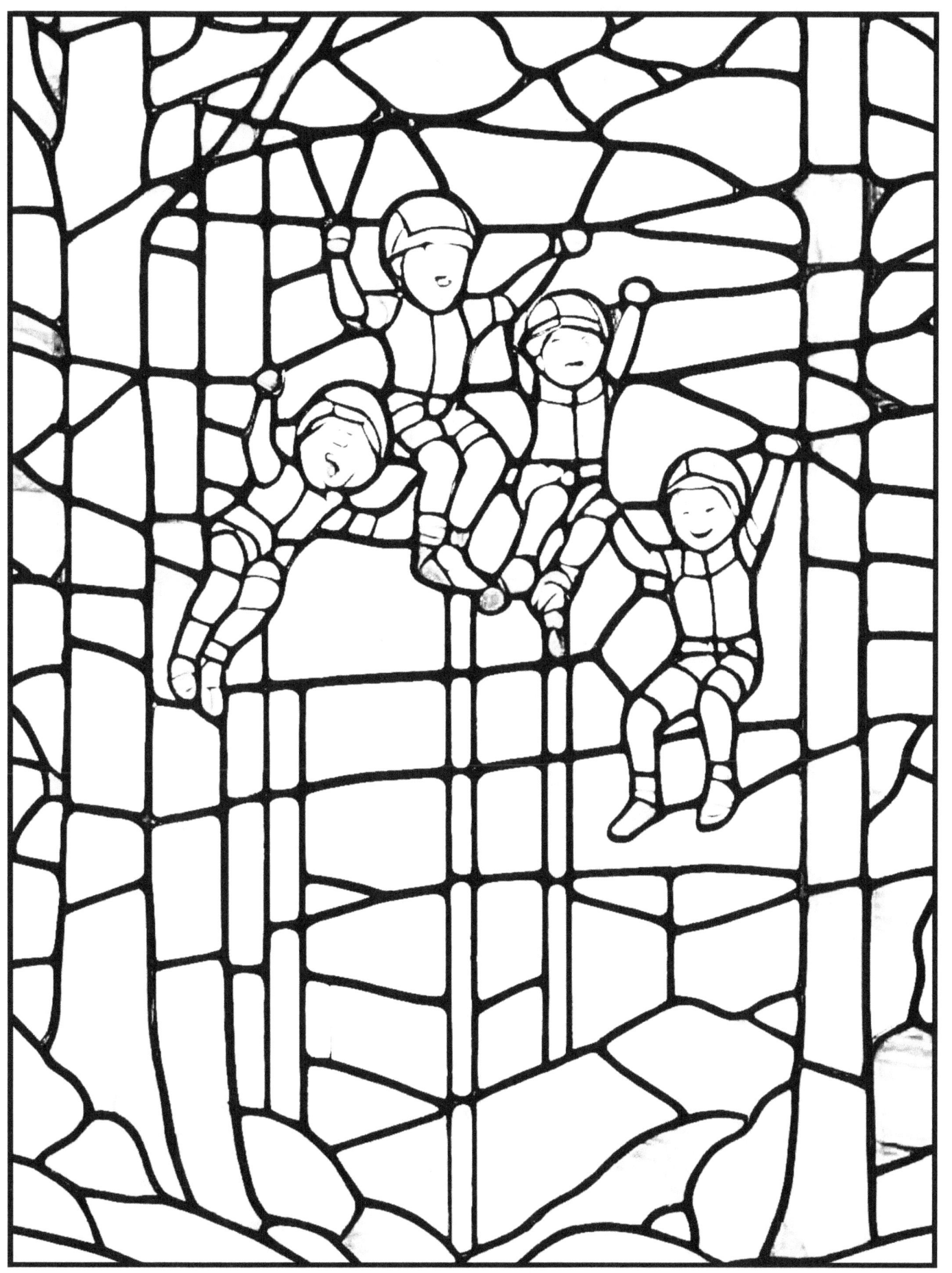

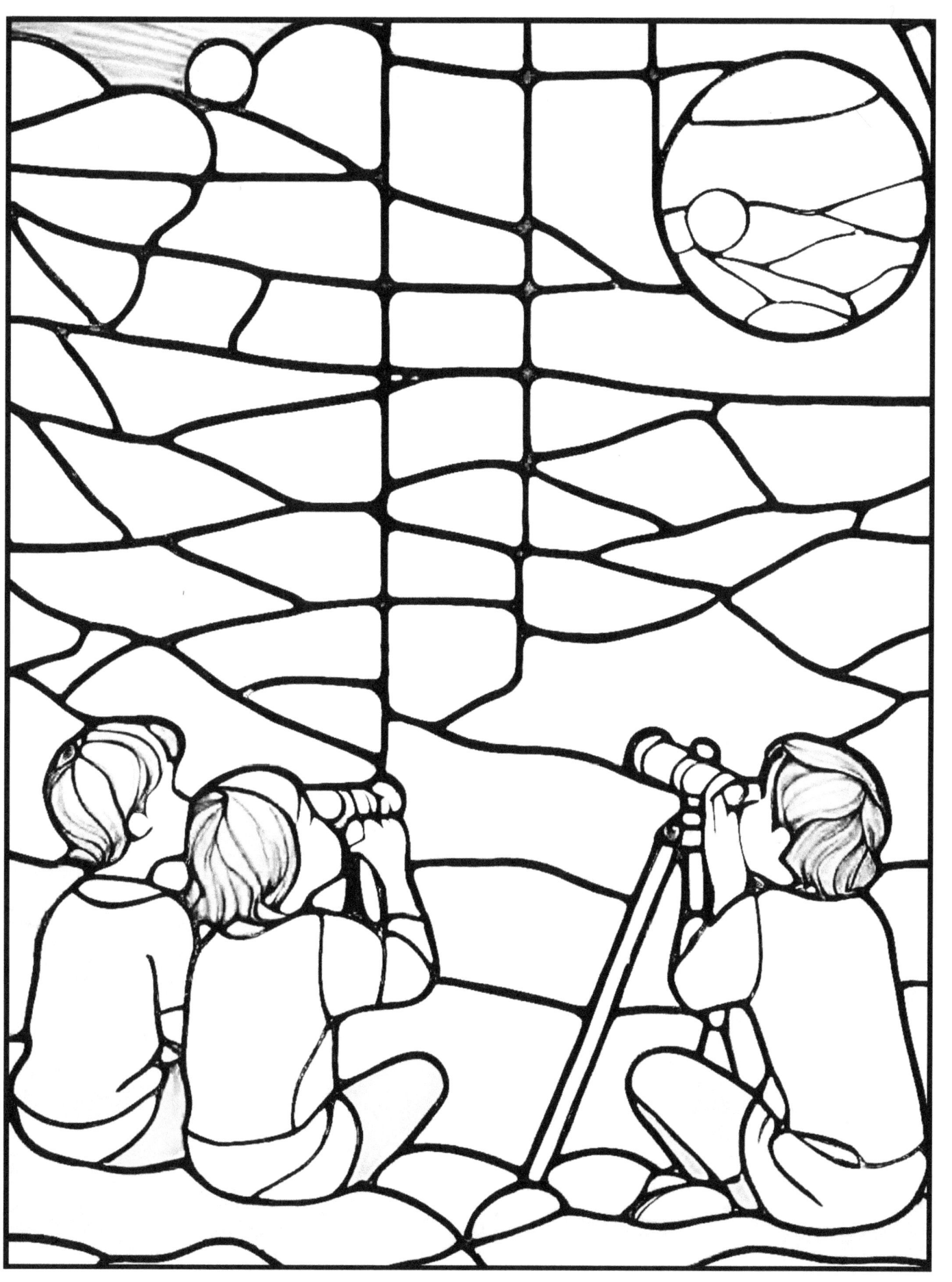

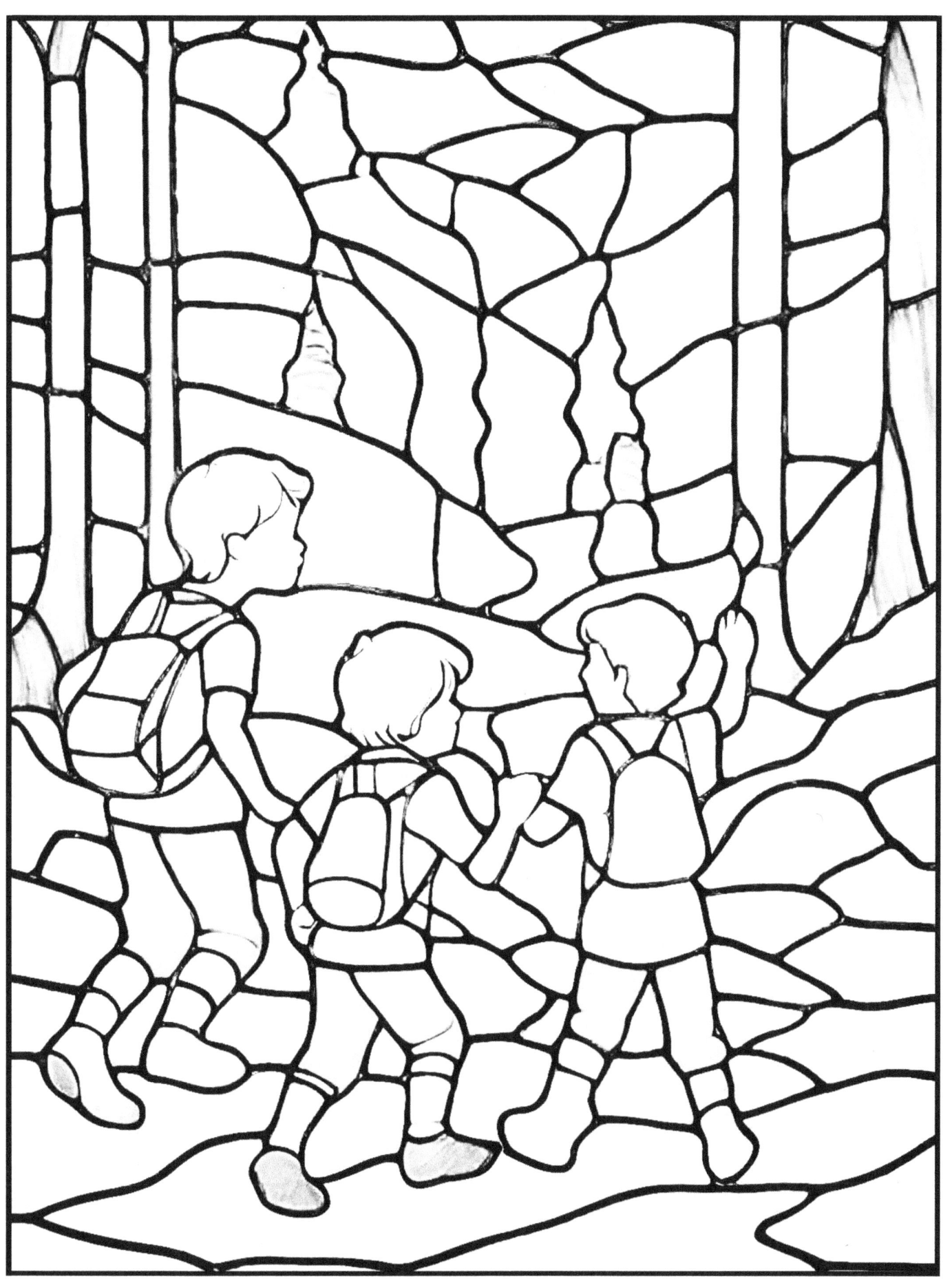

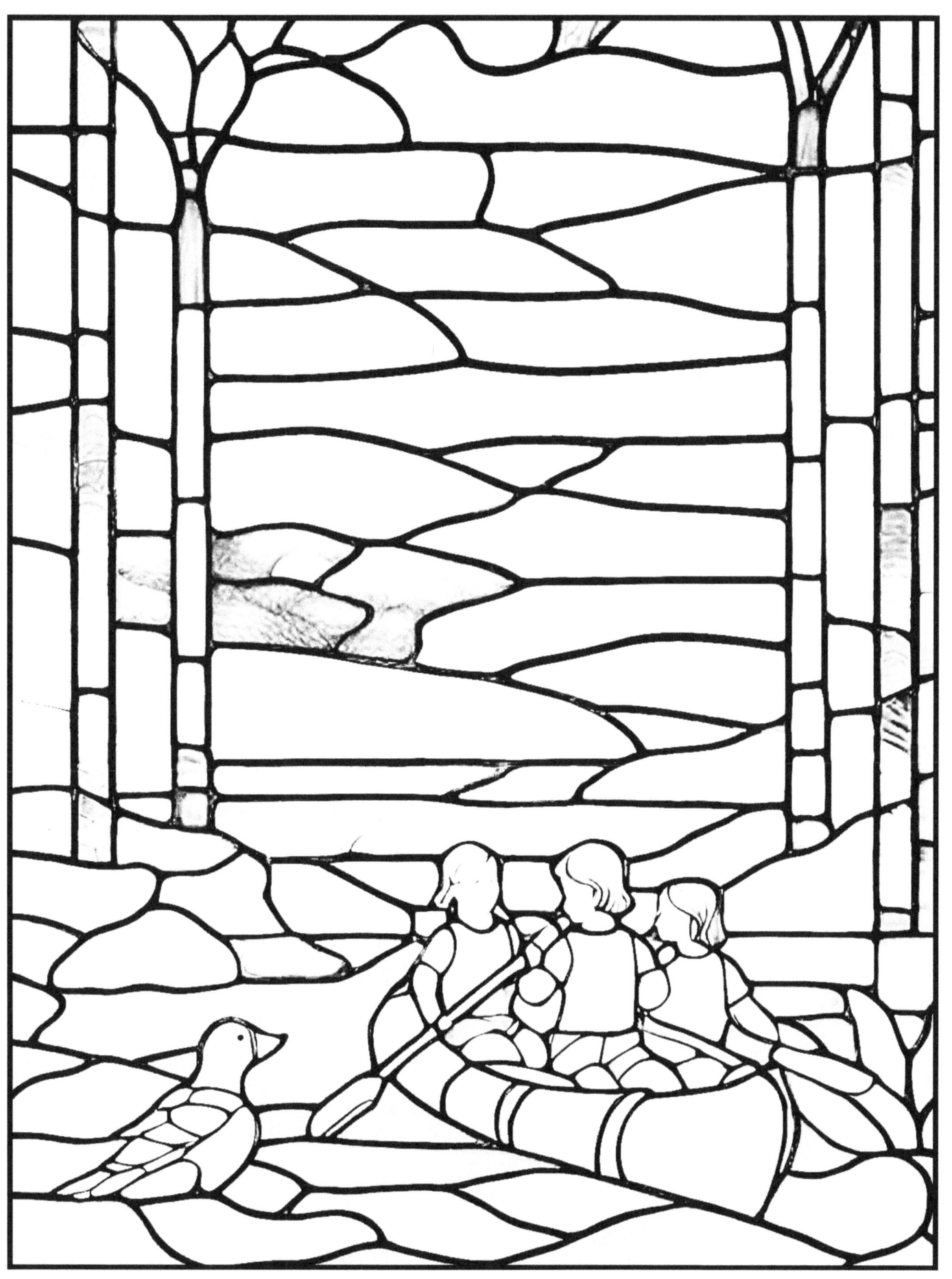

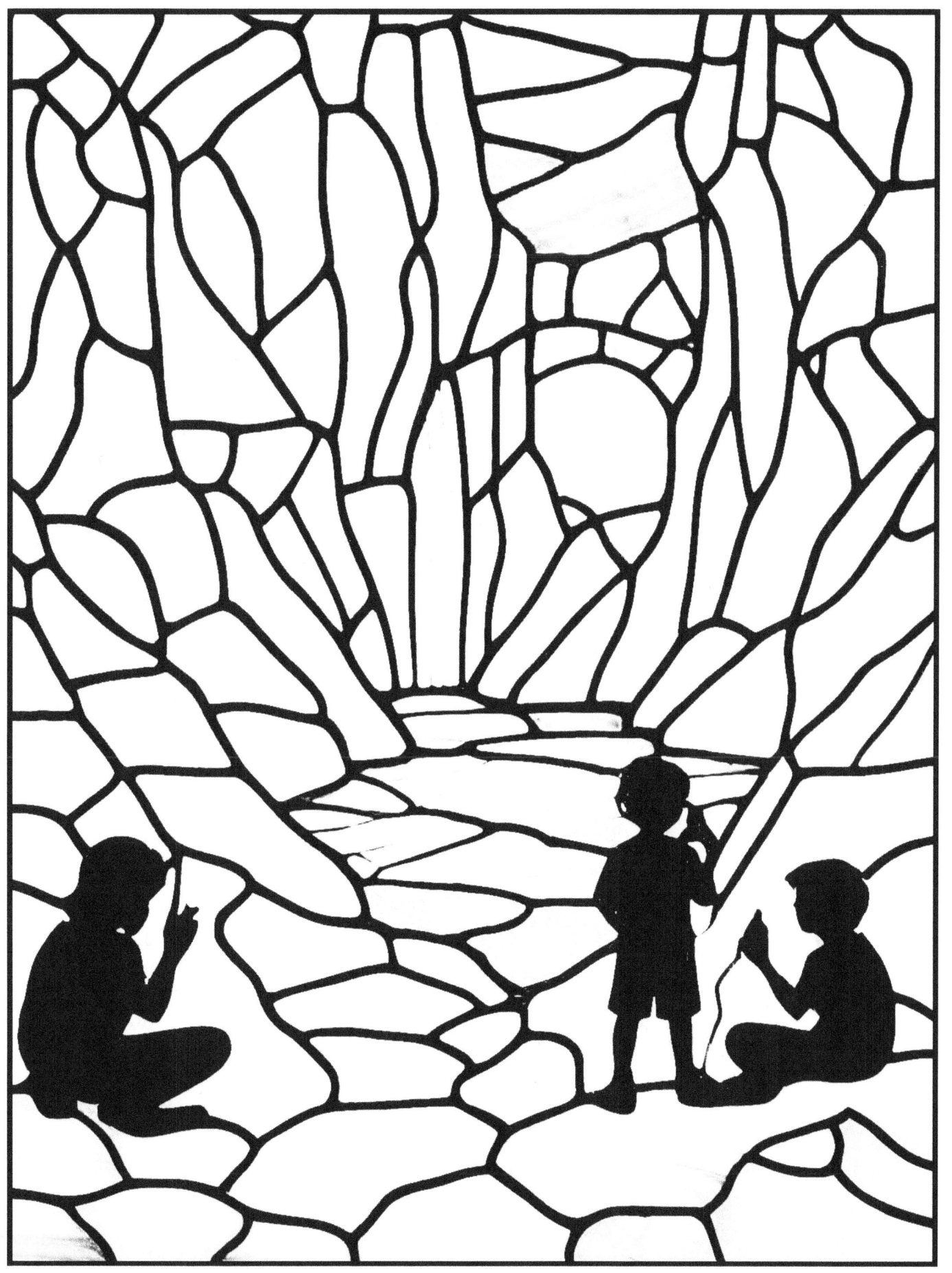

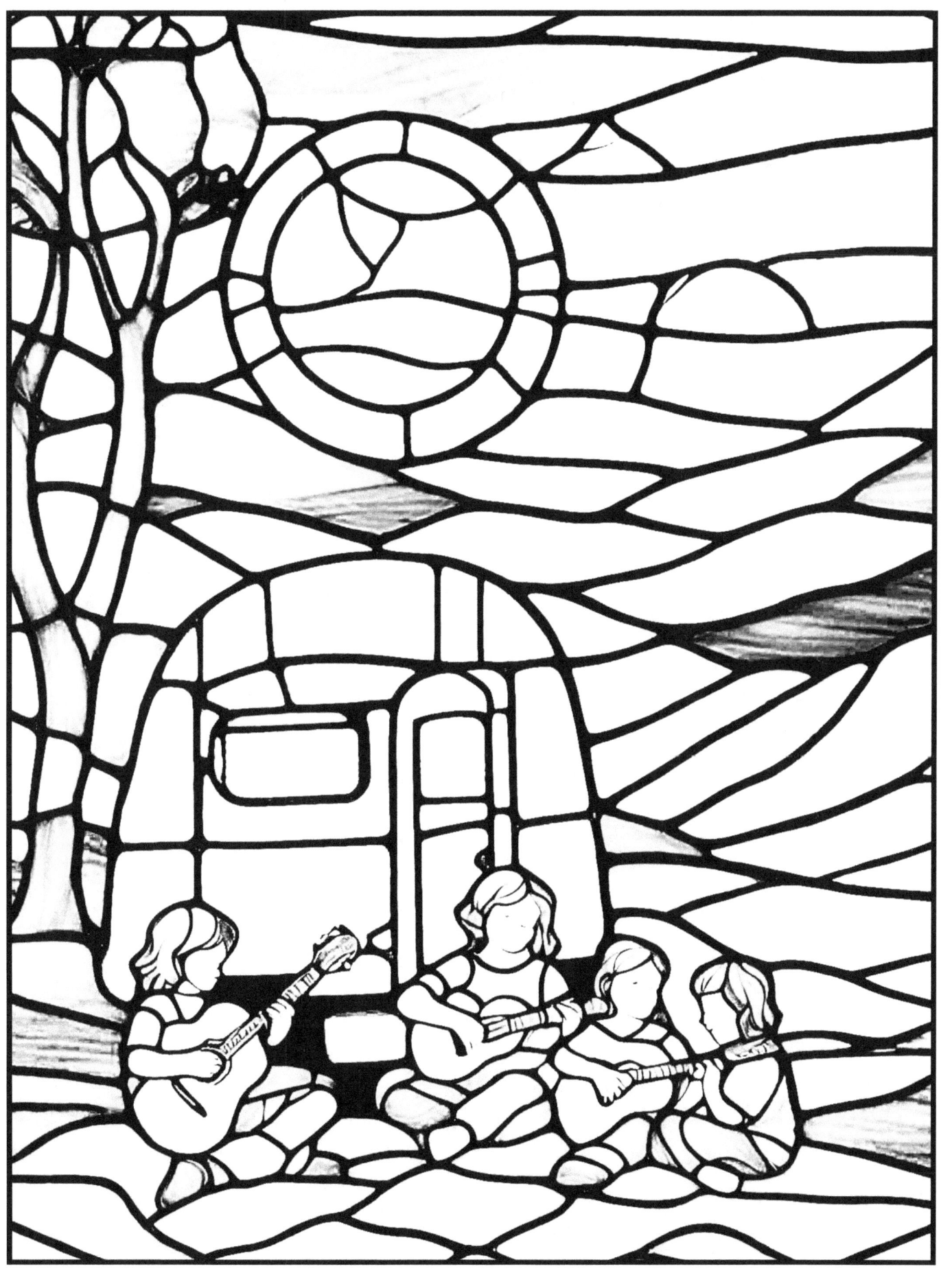

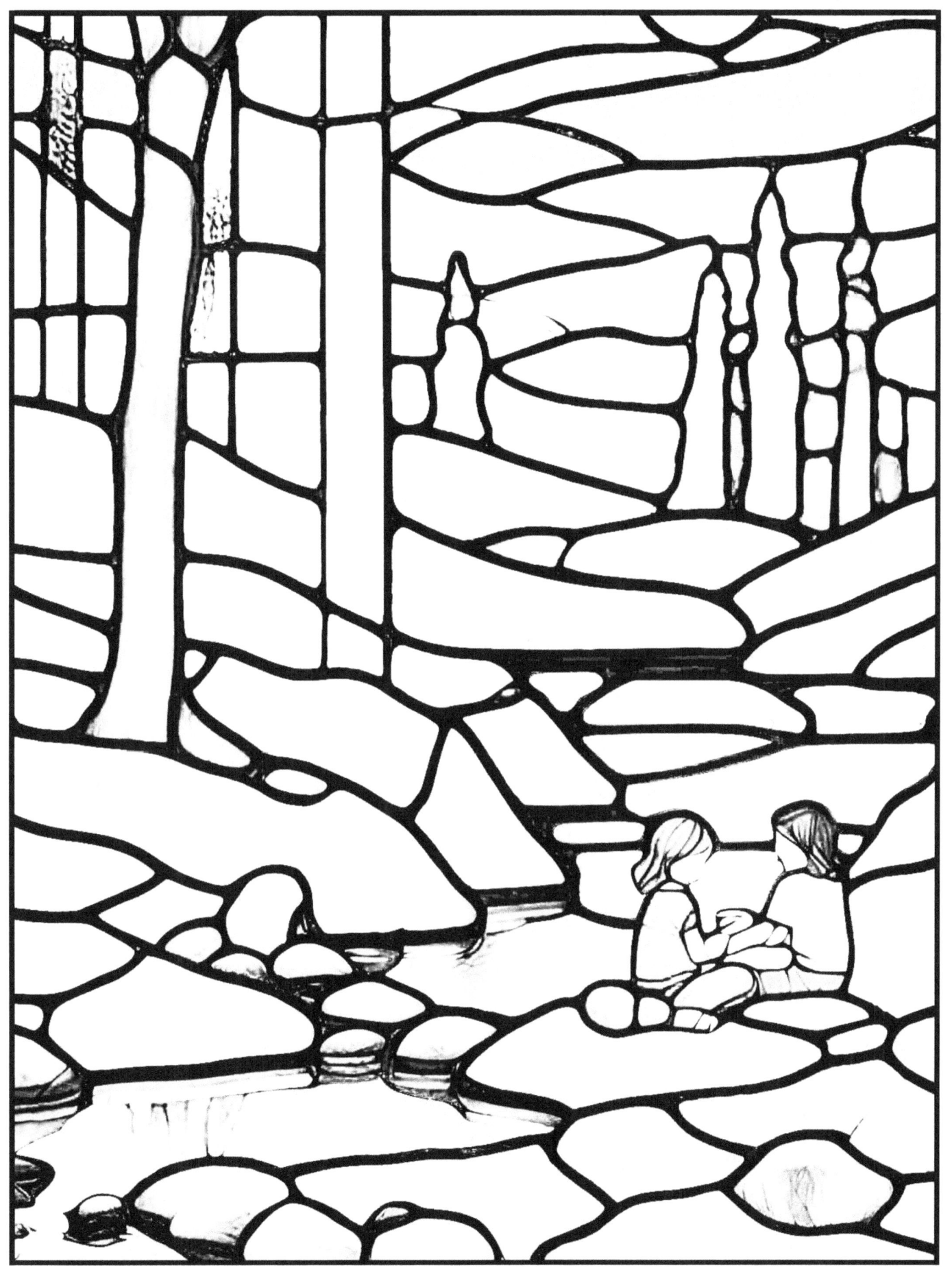

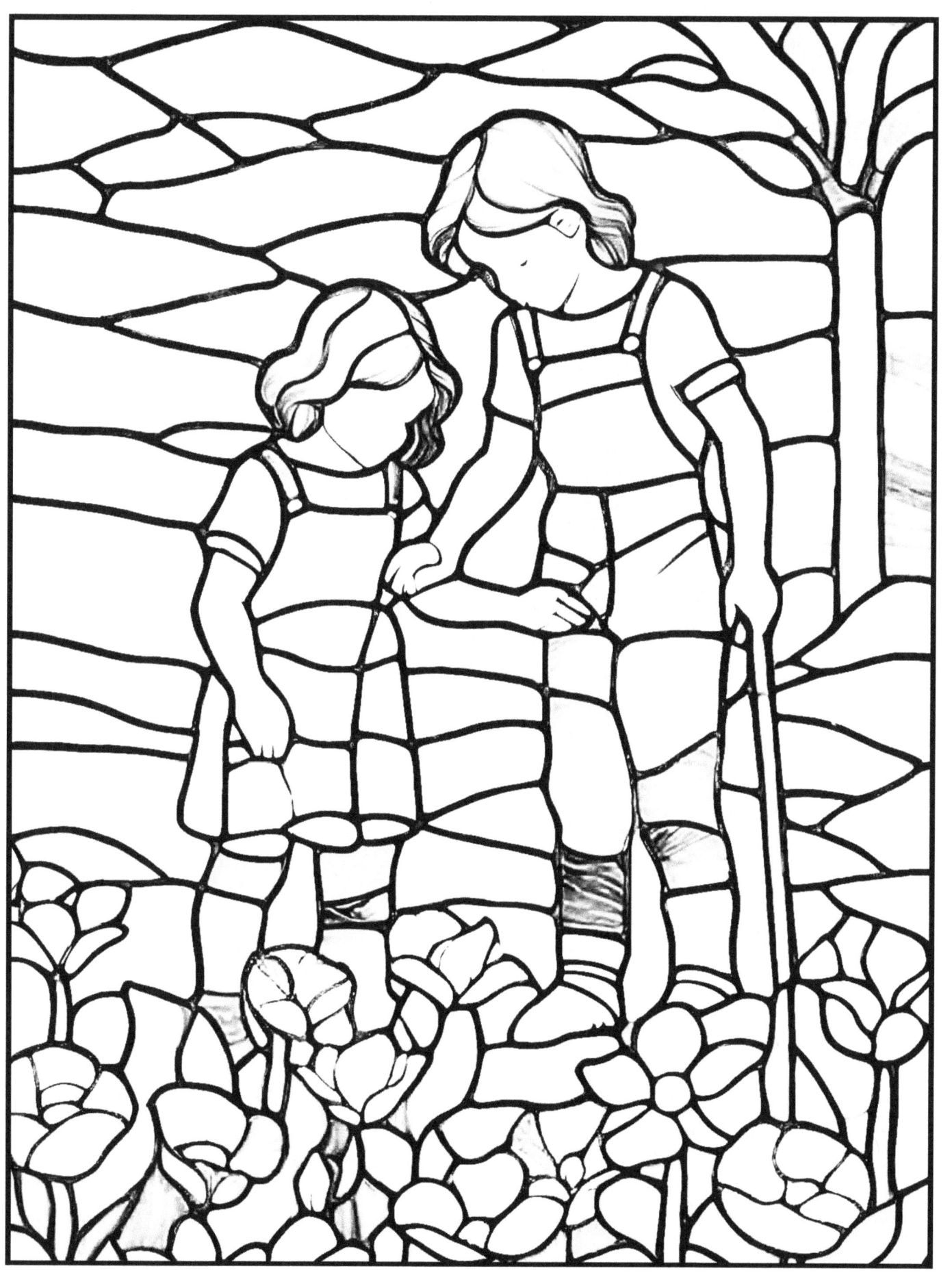

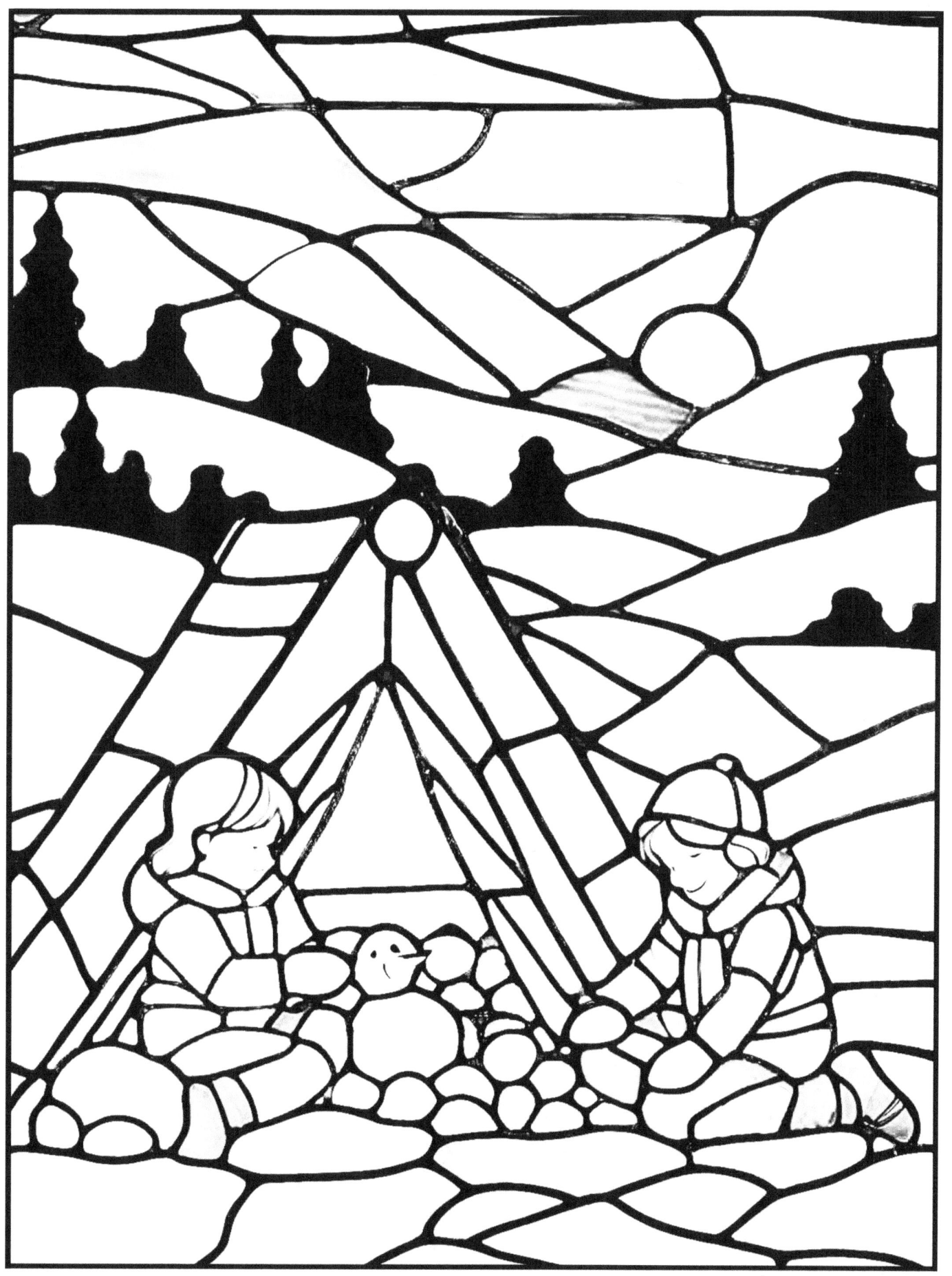

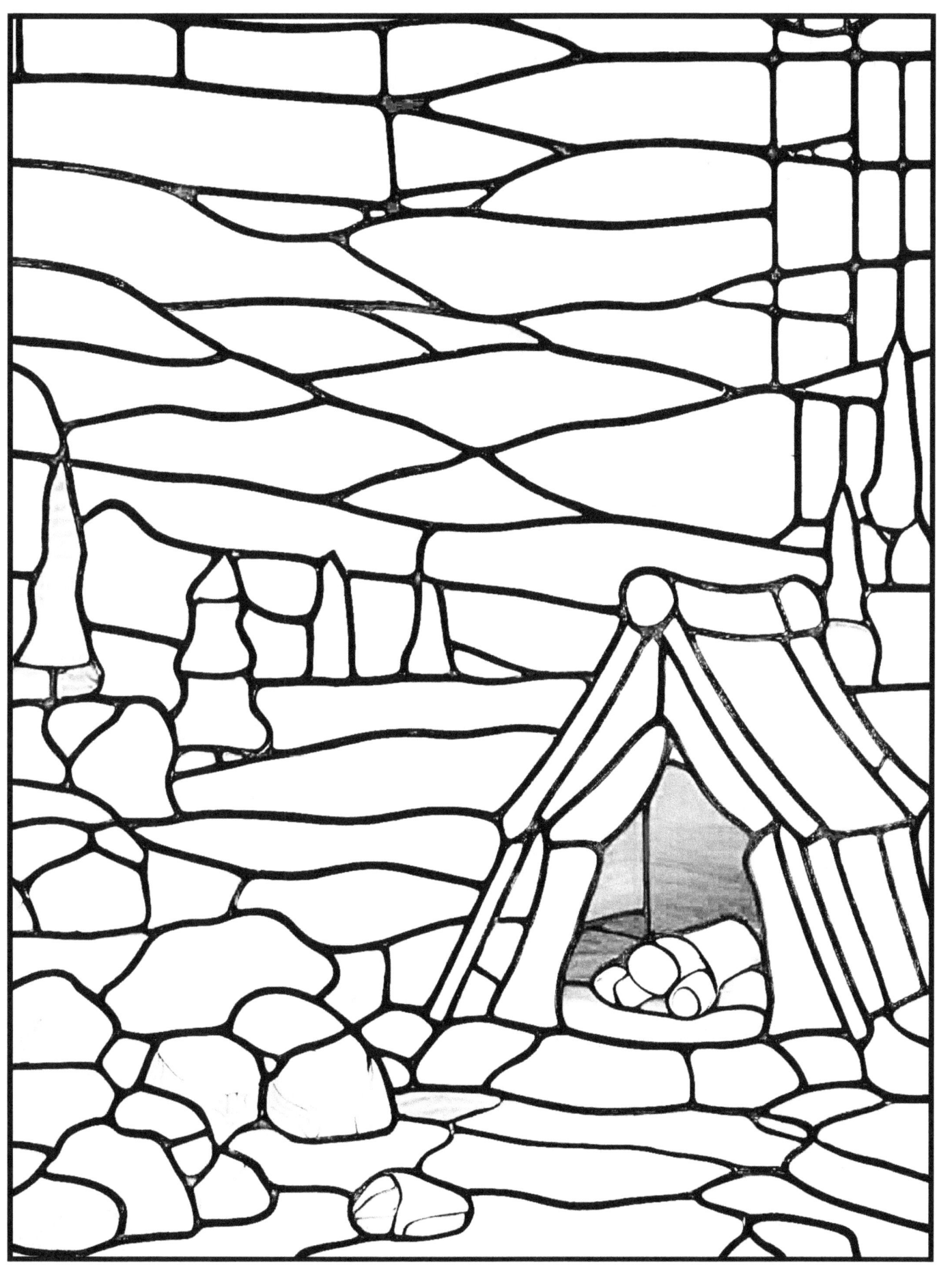

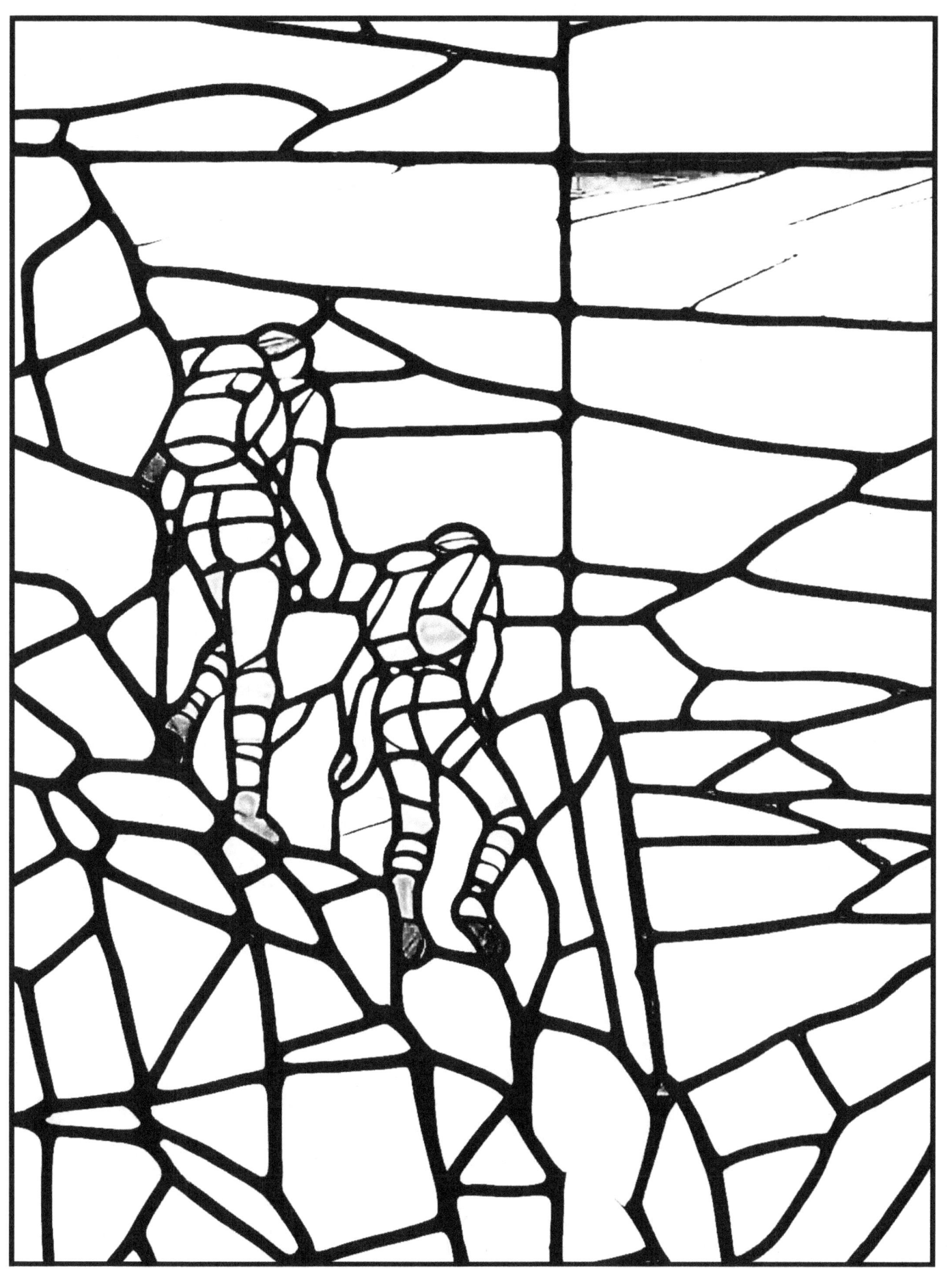

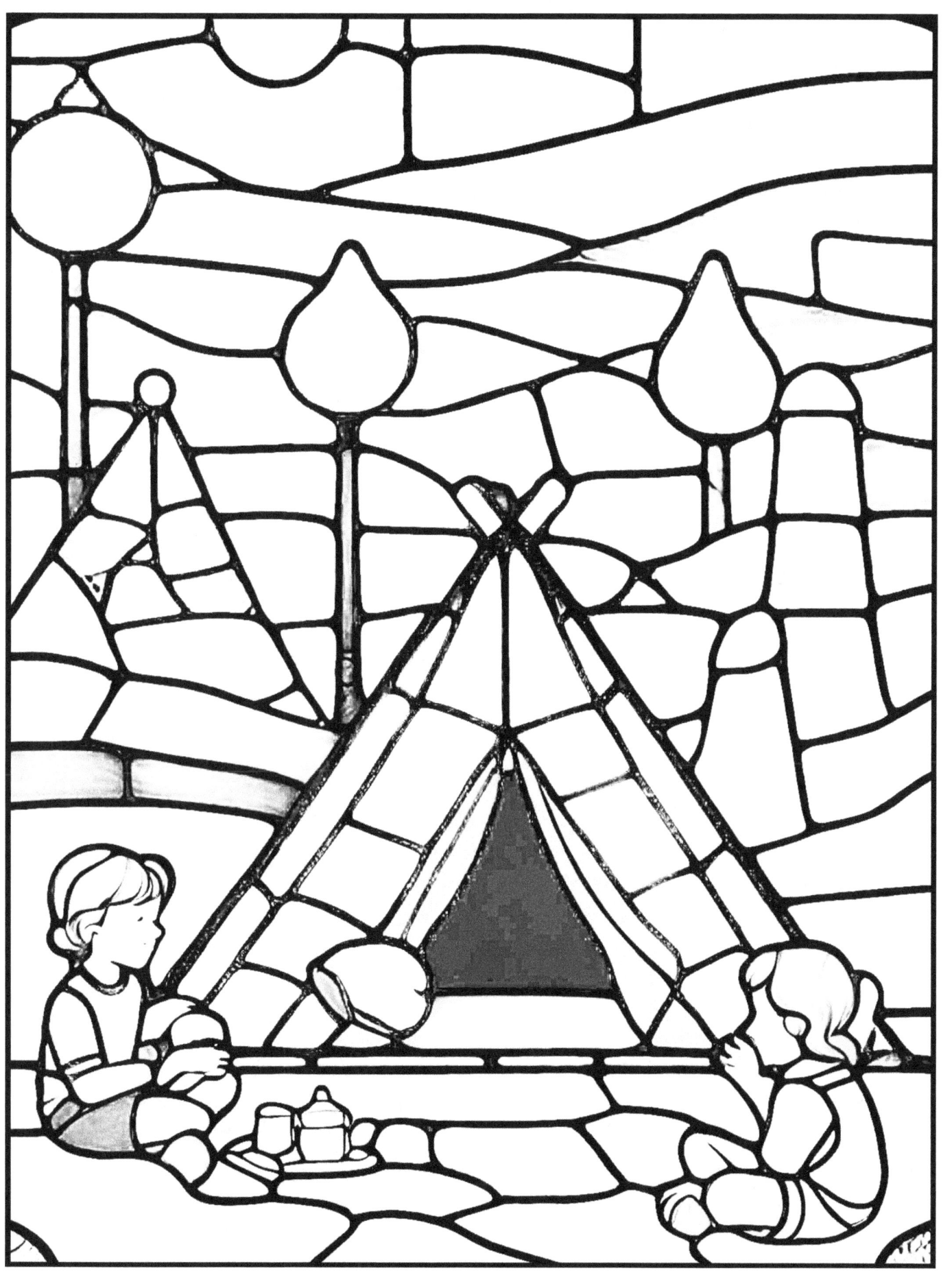

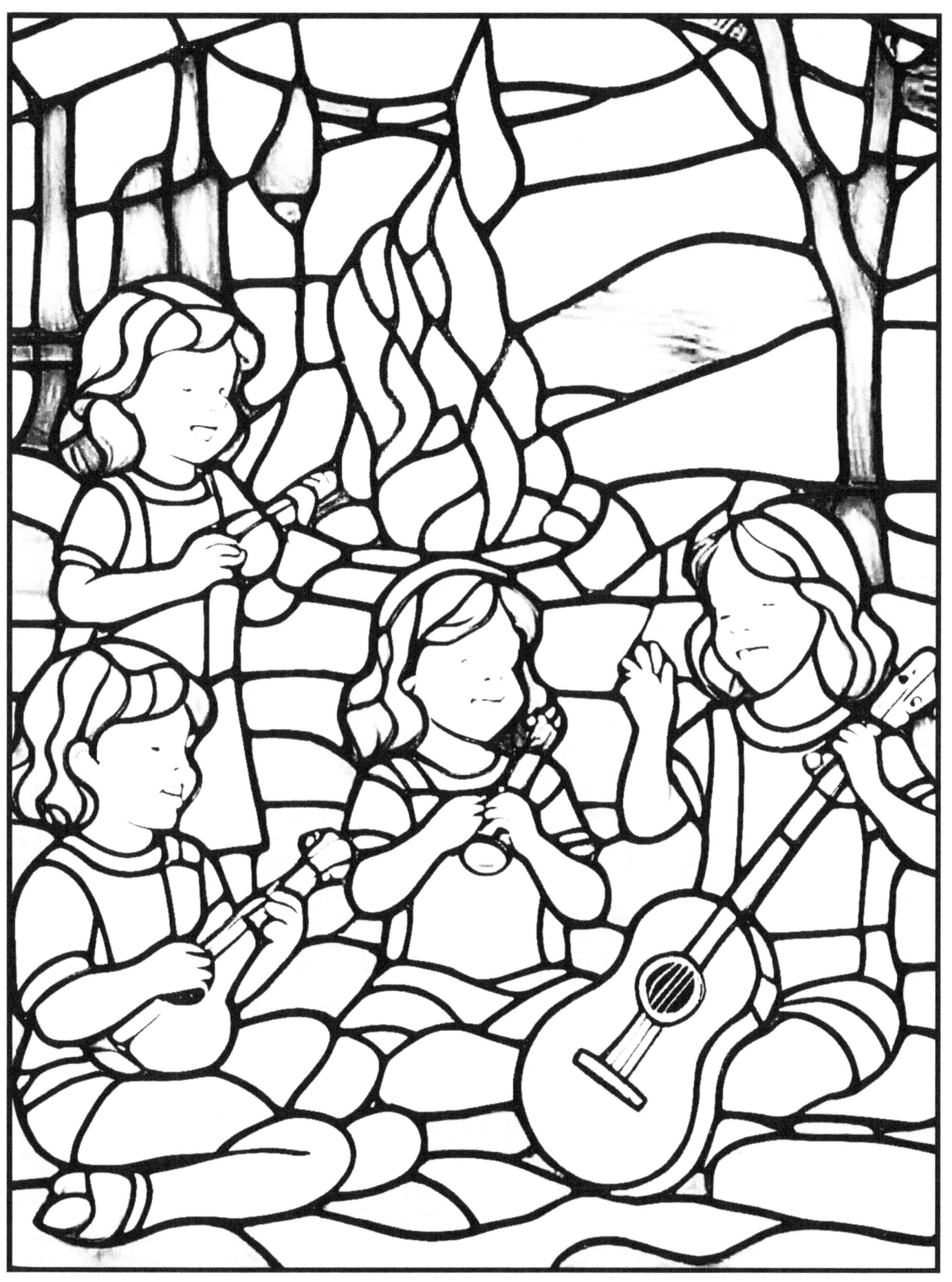

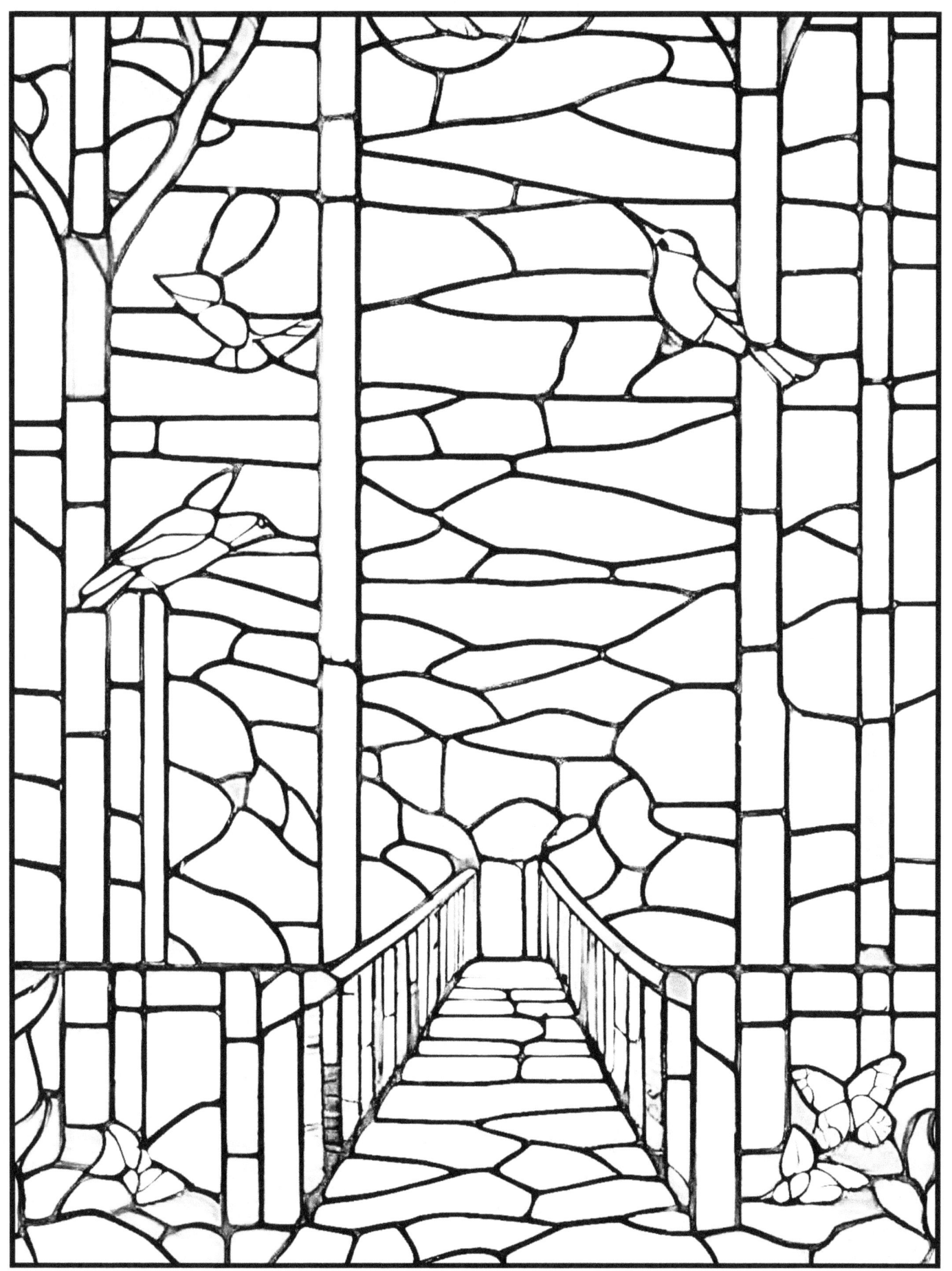

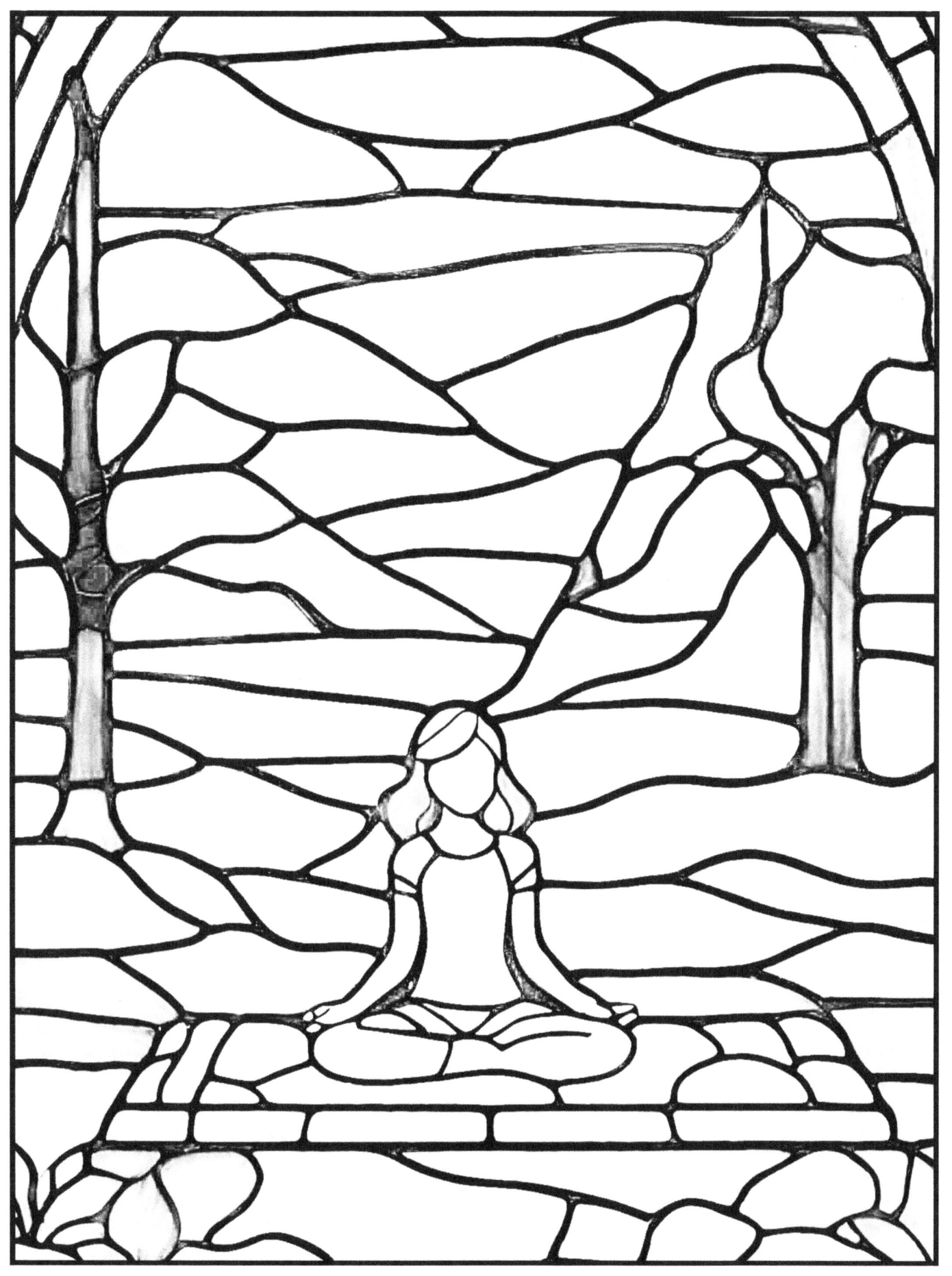

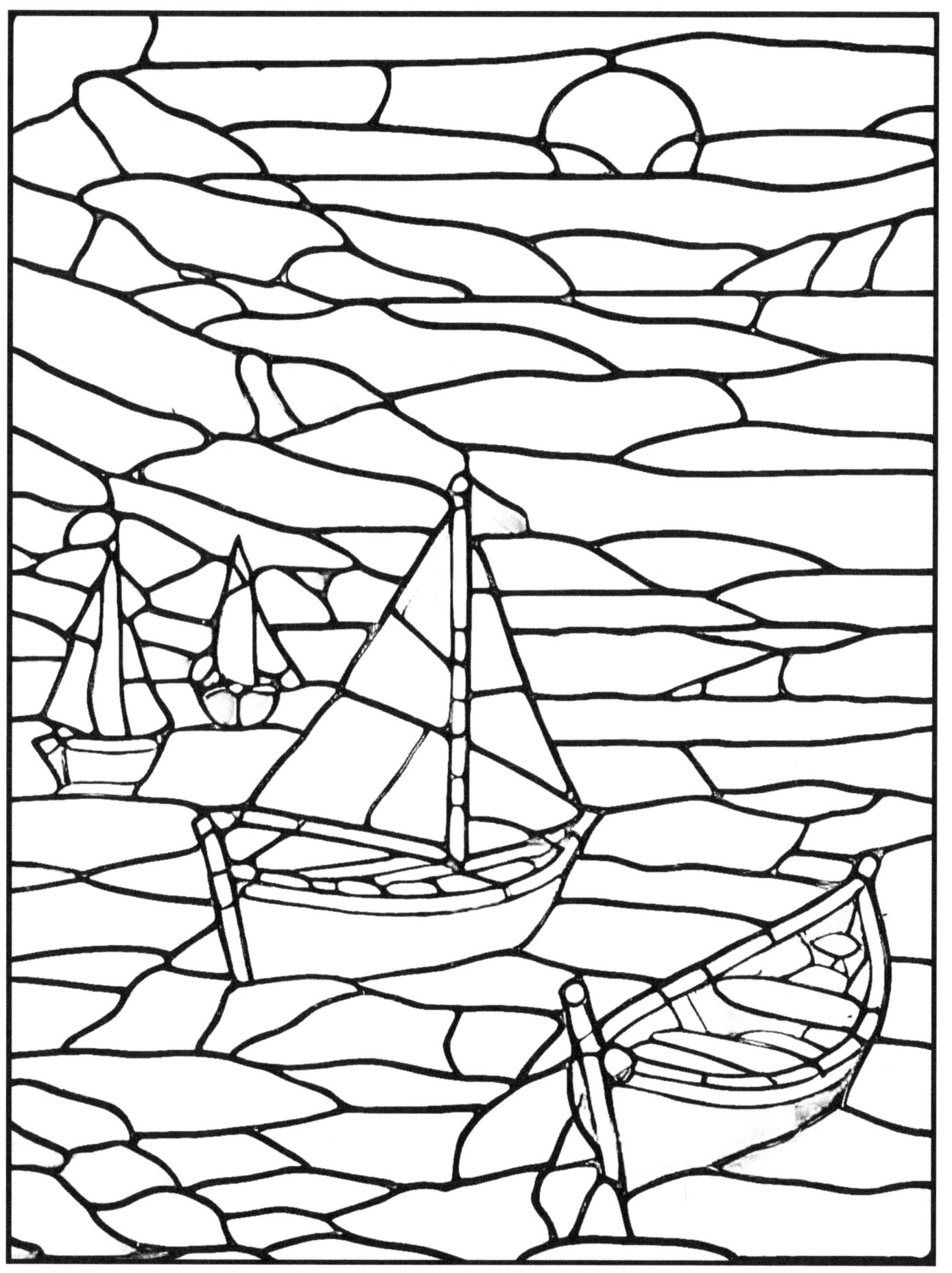

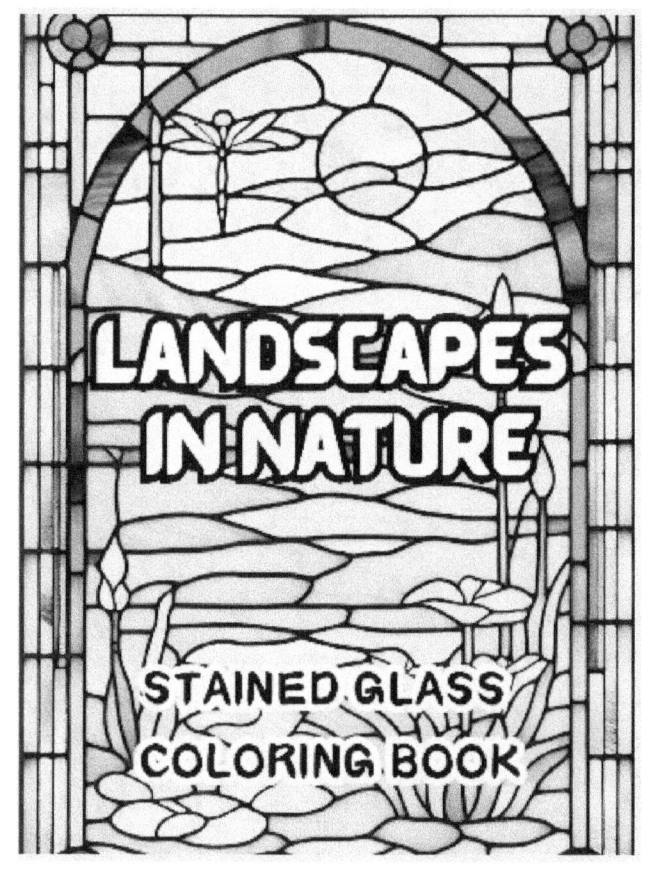
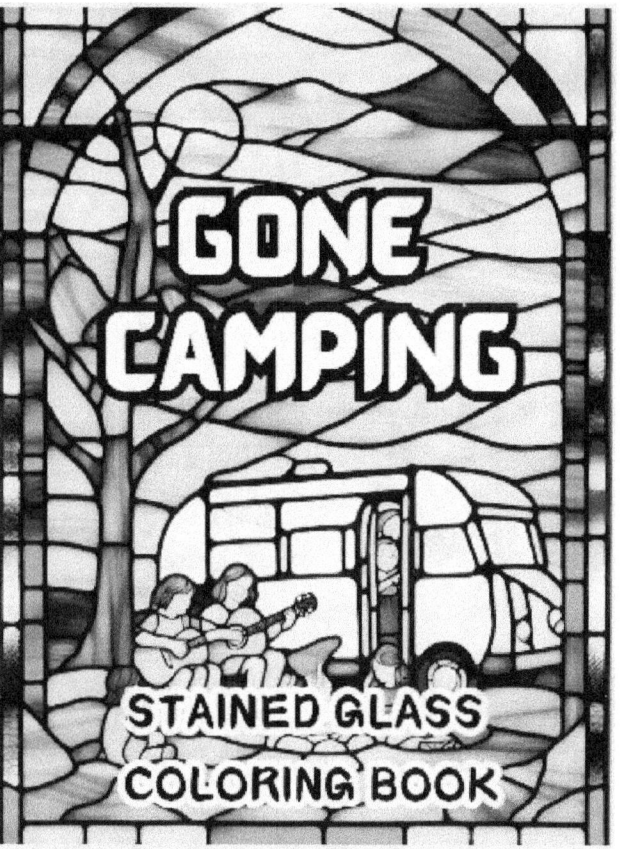

Thank you for choosing Camping Stained
Glass Coloring Book (Large Print).

Explore more stained glass coloring book
and other activity books on my Amazon
author page:

https://amazon.com/author/sylviarobins.